Better Boat Handling

Des Sleightholme has also written:

ABC for Yachtsmen
Fitting Out
Cruising
Old Harry's Bunkside Book
Up the Creek with Old Harry
This is Cruising
The Trouble with Cruising

Better Boat Handling

Des Sleightholme

SEVEN SEAS PRESS, INC.
NEWPORT, RI   02840

SEVEN SEAS PRESS, INC.

NEWPORT, RHODE ISLAND

Published by Seven Seas Press Inc.
Newport, Rhode Island 02840
Foreign Acquisitions Manager: Heather Campbell

Originally published in Great Britain by
Stanford Maritime Ltd
12–14 Long Acre, London WC2E 9LP

First published in the United States of America 1983
Copyright © by J. D. Sleightholme 1983

Jacket painting by Lawrence Bagley
Printed in the United States of America

Library of Congress Cataloguing in Publication Data
Sleightholme, J. D.
    Better boat handling.
    1. Ship handling. 2. Boats and boating.
    3. Seamanship. I. Title.
VK543.S57   1983   623.88′223   82-19210
ISBN 0-915160-30-7

1 3 5 7 9 HC/HC 0 8 6 4 2

Contents

What this Book is About

A new owner, having learned the basics of sailing and pilotage, henceforth will be learning by doing. He will face a series of new and taxing little problems and situations, each demanding of him skills he has not yet been able to acquire. This is why each nautical contretemps adds to his knowledge; each emergency increases his skill.

Each such situation also carries the risk that he will damage his boat or incur even more grave trouble. Most of these situations would not be emergencies if he already had thought about them and drilled himself in coping with them.

Our aim in this book is to jump the gun by setting up various boat handling and pilotage exercises designed to train an owner in the skills he is likely to need when emergencies of one sort or another arise. Naturally, any contrived, artificial situation lacks the immediacy of the real thing; moreover the real thing often happens without any warning. But if an owner can become the complete master of his own boat and if his mind already has chewed over some of the likely problems, the real thing, when it happens, is less likely to confuse him.

Each of the following chapters starts with several typical problem situations to illustrate the techniques likely to be needed. It then sets out to deal with their acquisition. Many of the practical exercises will have to be tackled when wind and tide or weather permit, but the reader who enjoys an afternoon sail will be able to please himself in what he tackles and when.

He will have to play fair and stick as closely as he can to the exercises at the end of each chapter. Nobody ever follows practice drills as closely as all that, of course, but the more often the reader tackles the boat handling exercises and the more often he mulls over the thoughts on emergency and decision-making, the more readily he will be able to cope with the real thing.

In devising these exercises in my own boat – which I thought I could handle pretty well, incidentally – I have learned a great deal more about her characteristics. Indeed, her handling ability in a fresh breeze under engine has forced me to adopt some new techniques which have saved me a lot of varnish work and a few blushes.

A good deal of emphasis is laid upon emergency in this book, but this need not dismay the newcomer to cruising at sea. Cruising is fun. The less it is marred by needless troubles, the more fun it becomes. There is delight to be had from handling a boat well – and being seen to handle her well.

JDS

CHAPTER I

Seamanship: Handling Under Auxiliary Engine

Situations

1 You are making for a vacant marina berth in a strange port and on a breezy day when the Dockmaster hails you and directs you to a different berth and one which you have already passed by. You'll either have to turn in a very narrow space or carry out the manoeuvre astern.

2 You are towing a dinghy under engine and against a strong river ebb. The current is rushing through crowded moorings. The towing painter parts (or is accidentally cast off) and the drifting dinghy will have to be recovered.

3 Motoring up a narrow creek with a fresh following wind. The creek narrows abruptly and it is too narrow to anchor among the moored craft. The yacht must be turned short in order to take her out again.

4 Approaching a jetty under power and with a following wind. She is carrying too much headway and she must be slowed. How will she behave if the engine is put full astern?

Originally, auxiliary engines were sufficiently powerful to push the boat along in a calm and manoeuvre in harbour; nowadays they are frequently big enough to give maximum designed speed at sea and still have a reserve of power. There is little point in trying to push a boat faster than her designed speed. All that happens is that she sits back on her stern and builds up a huge wave. Beyond this point the ratio of power needed for every extra half knot gained becomes totally uneconomical.

When it comes to manoeuvring under power, however, this extra reserve of boost is very useful. With the boat at a near standstill, heavy bursts of engine power can be used to jerk her stern round or to stop her quickly. In the crowded yacht harbours of today an inexperienced owner comes up against the problems of jockeying a boat around in confined spaces from the very beginning and it is for this reason that we are going to tackle power handling first of all.

A boat afloat never ceases to move. Even moored or at anchor she swings and turns to every breath of wind, and when she is under way (and she is said to be under way even when she is making no progress ahead or astern) she is subject to drift and to the influence of current. Only when she is under sail or power and water is flowing past her rudder is she under control. However, she need not be moving fast for her helmsman to have complete control of her and it is a mark of the expert that he can place his boat exactly where he wants her to be by dint of understanding her drift characteristics and her obedience to rudder and engine power.

If we had a state of perpetual tideless calm we would develop handling techniques as unvarying as those we use for garaging our cars. Imagine, though, having a garden gate which is forever shifting position, a slope which is never the same two days together, and a car which on occasion has a tendency to drift sideways. The approach to a marina berth can be almost as unpredictably tricky. On one day there may be a fresh cross-wind or a cross-current. On another day the wind is dead astern, or from ahead. On every separate occasion the helmsman will have to take stock and decide what tactic to employ and in order to do this he must know in advance exactly how his boat will behave. He may, for instance, know that his powerful engine has dramatic stopping power but that with his propeller biting astern the boat's stern will swing hard to port. If he is berthing port side to the jetty this may help him, but if he is berthing starboard side to it will generate all manner of trouble, with a following wind.

Wind drift varies from boat to boat. With a shallow draft and high topsides a boat may blow around like a cardboard box. Conversely, a boat with modest freeboard and a deep underwater profile drifts very little, but she may be one hell of a problem to turn tightly under power and almost impossible to control when going astern.

Almost all boats have one thing in common: left to drift they tend to turn their bows downwind. I once had a twin-keel cruiser that did this to the extreme and she would go romping off downwind the moment you cut the engine and released her tiller; most boats lie halfway. This weather-cocking tendency can be used to good effect once it is understood, but each boat is different and each calls for separate study. A long-keeled hull lying across the wind may be reluctant to have her bows rounded up into the wind while a short-keeled hull pinwheels easily. Some are easy to control astern and others are absolute pigs; some can be turned short in their own lengths by a hard burst ahead on full rudder; others have to be juggled around by going ahead and astern by degrees.

While the smaller yacht can be berthed by dint of boathook, boot and *bonhomie*, by being aimed at a berth, deflected into it and stopped by means of a huge burst astern, the same tactics applied to a bigger boat or in windy weather can lead to a horrifyingly expensive smash-up.

ASSESSING THE BOAT

An old hand weighs up a boat strange to him more or less instinctively, taking stock of freeboard, rig, hull type and engine power. He will have a shrewd idea what to expect in any given set of conditions, but he still won't push his luck until he has had the helm in his hands for a while. Under power he will detect any tendency for the boat to pull against her rudder and he will soon get an idea of her turning circle.

An auxiliary sailing yacht under power is subject to a number of forces. The side-paddle effect of the propeller is a major one and few craft, once the tiller is released, will continue to move ahead in a straight line. Some may go off on a long shallow curve while others begin with a gradual curving off which increases and tightens. That same twin-keel cruiser of mine had this trick to a dangerous degree and the first time I tried leaving the helm for a quick trip to the foredeck she nearly flung me overboard.

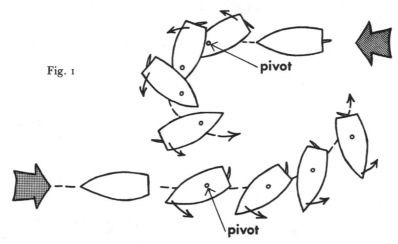

Fig. 1

A boat moving ahead pivots around a position about one-third of her length back from the bows, but when moving astern this pivot point moves aft to a point close to her stern; the tendency mentioned earlier to point her stern into the wind therefore becomes more dominant (Fig. 1). The following exercises will illustrate these factors.

EXERCISE 1   Feeling the helm

We will assume that you will have to motor some distance to a suitable exercise area of clear water. Proceeding at about half speed, gauge the tiller pressure by holding it with one finger, first on one side then the other, and note which way she tends to throw her bows. Increase speed and repeat. As soon as you have completely clear water around you and nothing coming up astern, reduce speed to half again and let go of the tiller completely (warn your crew). Repeat at full speed.

EXERCISE 2   Stopping

This exercise should be carried out in calm or light conditions, if possible. Make a drift mark consisting of a child's ball in a vegetable net, ballasted by any weight (a stone will do) hung on about six feet of cord. Since the drift mark will be subject to the same tidal drift as the yacht, tideless conditions will be simulated for the following manoeuvres (Fig. 2A). Drop the mark and motor away from it, upwind for perhaps 200 yards, then motor full speed towards the mark. Cut the engine as the mark comes abeam and note the distance travelled before losing all way. If there is any wind, repeat this exercise into the wind, then across the wind.

Recover the drift mark and by adding a suitable length of cord for three times the depth of water, anchor it and repeat the above. This is assuming that there is a tidal current of sufficient strength to make it worthwhile: this being so, you will be able to gauge the true effect of current plus and minus boat speed in terms of stopping without putting the engine astern.

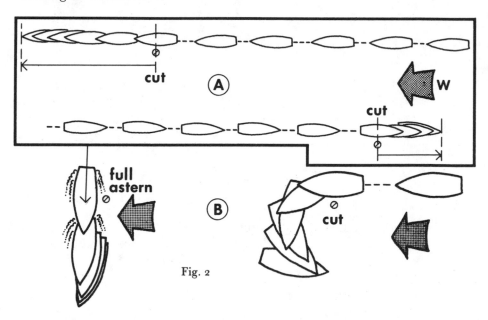

Fig. 2

EXERCISE 3   Loss of way when rounding up

With the mark still moored, approach at full speed to bring it abeam one boat's length to port. Apply full port rudder (note *rudder*) while simultaneously cutting the engine. Note how close the yacht rounds up to the mark and what happens thereafter; how quickly she stops. Repeat to starboard (Fig. 2B).

You will now have some idea of how far the boat carries her way, with and against wind and current, and how fast she loses her way after cutting the engine and applying full rudder. Now we must find out how she behaves with engine astern in slow and crash stops.

EXERCISE 4 Stopping by reversing propeller

If there is more than a knot of current running it is worth recovering the anchored mark and rigging it as a drift mark again because it is important to be able to assess engine stopping power uninfluenced by current. If there is more than a very light breeze make the first approach run across the wind and as the buoy comes abeam throttle back, engage astern, and open up to full revs smoothly; never bang from full ahead to full astern. Note the stopping distance, also what happens to the boat's stern. With a clockwise (right-handed) rotation of the propeller when in ahead, going astern will tend to paddle her stern to port; just how much it does this is very important to know. With a fresher breeze on the beam this effect will be either increased or diminished, so therefore make further runs into and with the wind. If time permits and the current makes a significant difference, repeat yet again with the mark moored.

At this stage we should take a closer look at this whole theory of propeller side-paddle effect. When a boat is stationary a burst of engine with a high-revving propeller churns the water giving a cavitation effect; then, as the boat begins to move the blades begin to bite and perform efficiently.
A bigger propeller turning more slowly bites more quickly but it also has a much more pronounced side-paddle effect. The upper blade of a propeller as it turns is in less resisting water than the lower and this produces a sideways force. A very rough analogy would be to imagine a boat on dry land with a wheel replacing the propeller and supporting the stern off the ground. If the wheel is turned clockwise the stern will be moved to the right, anticlockwise it moves to the left (Fig. 3).

Fig. 3

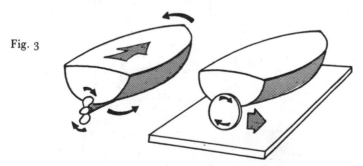

So, with a clockwise or right-handed propeller the stern kicks to starboard when the engine is engaged ahead and to port when in astern. Most yachts have right-handed propellers. The rotation is always identified when viewed from astern looking forward, and since the best *aide memoires* seem to be those which are a bit vulgar I make no apologies for this one: 'A kick ahead gives a kick up the ASS' (ahead-stern-starboard). It isn't much trouble to reverse the thinking for the astern kick ASP (astern-stern-port).

EXERCISE 5   Turning in a fresh breeze

To get any real benefit from this exercise the breeze should be Force 4–5 or more. The typical modern fin keel and skeg rudder sailing cruiser can be turned on her heel within her own length in moderate conditions.

Make up a second mark and anchor the pair of them in line across the wind and about two lengths apart. Position the yacht between them and beam-on to the wind, as stationary as possible. Put the rudder hard over to turn her into the wind and give her a short, hard burst ahead, cutting it as the boat gathers headway. The intention is to gauge the side-kick, boosting the bows round without making too much headway. Try several such bursts ahead. Try the exercise with the wind on both the port and the starboard beam and observe whether there is a tendency for the boat to turn into wind under this burst of power more readily to port (ASS), as should be the case with a right-handed propeller (Fig. 4).

With a little imagination the two buoys can represent the walls of a dock or a marina lane and with a boat that turns tightly under full power on a full rudder this is obviously the best tactic to adopt, but it takes some nerve. Unless you have full confidence in your boat's turning ability in all weights of wind, the looming menace of a stone wall drawing closer by the second can cause you to dither – with possible dire consequences.

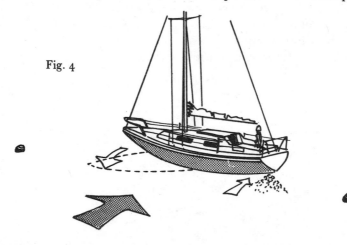

Fig. 4

EXERCISE 6   Backing and filling

In engine terms, backing and filling describes the alternate bursts ahead and astern which are sometimes used in an attempt to turn short. In anything of a fresh breeze they almost always fail, but it is well worth finding out how your own boat behaves (Fig. 5).

Fig. 5

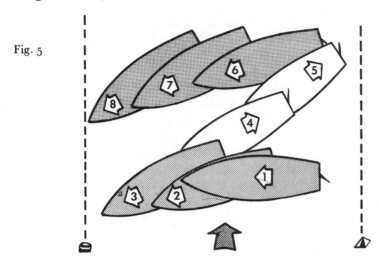

Again lying between the marks in a fresh breeze, this time starting with the wind on the port beam, start with rudder full port and a burst ahead, letting the stern get its kick to starboard but cutting the revs as soon as the boat begins forging hard ahead. Now give her a hard burst astern, building up the revs smoothly, though, to minimise the tendency of the stern to kick to port thus undoing any advantage gained with that first kick ahead (ASS). In theory the boat can be allowed to gather a little sternway and the rudder can be turned to starboard, taking her stern to starboard. The odds are that this won't happen. Her stern will try to weathercock upwind to port. When moving astern it usually takes a good long stretch before the rudder takes effect – if it has any effect at all in that sort of wind. This ahead-astern manoeuvre can be repeated again and again. It *may* be successful but most likely the only result will be a gradual sideways progress downwind. The true value of this exercise is that it teaches a great deal about your boat's aptitudes in a fresh breeze, and maybe acts as a warning not to rely on backing and filling in a tight spot.

EXERCISE 7   Turning stern to wind

As already mentioned, most modern boats can be turned ahead within their own length or little more, even in a fresh breeze, but if there is any doubt of this and if the manoeuvre in the previous exercise fails, how *can* she be turned short upwind?

Many fin and skeg rudder hulls handle astern with great accuracy, and remembering the tendency for a boat to weathercock her stern into the wind in any case it is often far easier to go astern, rudder turned upwind, and go stern first out of the predicament. Before one relies on this manoeuvre, though, it is important to explore handling characteristics astern in a smart breeze.

Again lying with the port beam to wind and between the marks, give her full port rudder and full astern. If she can't quite complete the turn before fouling the mark astern, start off with the bows fairly close to the opposite mark. Once she begins to feel her rudder and her stern is dead into wind, ease the tiller amidships; glance over your shoulder to note the swing of the bows, because the pivot point now being near the stern, it will be the bows that swing while the stern follows the rudder. Try to hold a straight course. The weight of water piling against the rudder will cause it to swing hard over, either way, of its own accord, once the blade is allowed to deviate from amidships.

Try, if possible, to steer the yacht in a wide figure-of-eight. If it is possible to do this then you will know that you have excellent control going astern and the knowledge will sooner or later get you out of a scrape.

EXERCISE 8   Using the wind

By now the reader (having mystified observers to the point of desperation) will have a pretty good idea of what his boat under power will do for him, and of the degree of effect the wind has on his manoeuvres. There are several classic turning manoeuvres which make full use of wind effect (Fig. 6).

A. Wind on starboard beam To turn short and reverse direction (go back the way you've come), begin by sticking her bows upwind on full starboard rudder. Next pull straight astern downwind, applying port rudder to cock her stern to port a little, and finally go hard ahead applying starboard rudder to bring her on course.

Fig. 6

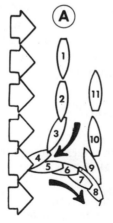
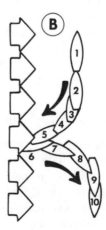

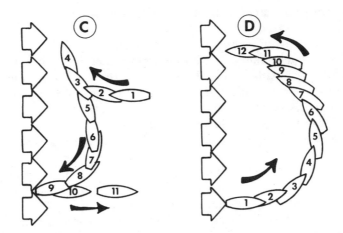

B. Wind on the port beam Using the weathercock effect of stern into wind, go astern on full port rudder until her stern is full into the wind, then ahead on full starboard rudder.

C. Wind dead ahead To turn so as to bring the wind dead astern, apply full starboard rudder until her bows have begun to pay off. Then put the engine astern on full port rudder, allowing the stern to weathercock up-wind. When her stern is well up-wind, go ahead again and straighten her up.

D. Wind dead astern In a strong wind and with a boat which has a poor turning-into-wind ability there is no simple answer if turning space is limited. In a channel one is best advised to hug one shore before beginning a turn on full rudder, gunning the engine hard as the turn begins. If, by the time you have reached mid-channel the bows have not begun to swing up into the wind, there will be some doubt whether you'll make it. If the boat has a tighter turning circle ahead to port (ASS effect) the turn *must* be started from close to the starboard side of the channel. If she still can't do it *don't* try backing and filling. The only resort is to let go the anchor with just enough scope to hold, swing on it and recover it as you go ahead into the wind. It is far less cumbersome a method than it sounds.

EXERCISE 9   Tight circling

If the wind happens to be fresh, Force 5 or above, turning into the wind sorts the sheep from the goats. A fair idea of the sort of performance a boat will put up can be gained by holding the helm hard over and circling ahead, first at slow then cruising revs and finally flat out, to port and starboard. In moderate conditions the average modern hull locks herself into a circle about $1\frac{1}{4}$–$1\frac{1}{2}$ boat lengths in diameter. A poor windward turner will describe an ellipse rather than a circle, longer on her poor turning side and perhaps only performing acceptably at full speed. The acid test is to start from lying stopped and drifting beam-on.

It is better to carry out all of this programme of exercises on the same day, in the same set of weather conditions, and perhaps repeat them in different conditions on another occasion.

If the yacht has a left-handed propeller then of course the various manoeuvres explained will have to be reversed, e.g. the stern will tend to throw to port going ahead and to starboard astern. There are other points to discover also, such as the effect on steering which may occur in a smaller cruiser when the helmsman leaves the helm and moves forward to the bows – a frequent cause of the lone sailor missing his mooring!

Although this chapter has dealt with handling under power alone, there are occasions and there are boats which can be better turned into wind with the aid of the mainsail, or in the case of yawls or ketches with the aid of the mizzen. Long-keeled craft in particular may benefit by this method, but as always it is a matter for individual experiment.

Before concluding the chapter one important point must be added. In legal definition a sailing vessel with sails set but also under engine power becomes a *power driven vessel*. In right-of-way situations she must thus behave as a power driven vessel, giving way according to the rights of other vessels. At night she must show the lights appropriate to a power vessel but in daytime, with sails set and drawing, it may not be apparent to other craft that she is under engine also and all manner of ducking and dodging may ensue, maybe even collision.

By day she must, by law, wear aloft a black cone shape hoisted point downwards forward of the mast and in a position where it can be seen (not always easy). In truth very few yachts comply with this regulation and for that matter a great many owners are not even aware of their responsibility to do so. In any case it is possible to reveal the fact that you are under engine by using mainsail only or by letting the sheet fly. The fact that you are seen to keep going at much the same speed with all sails a-shake will reveal the truth to any observant and experienced skipper nearby. Nevertheless, should a collision occur you would be in the wrong.

CHAPTER II

Handling Under Power – Dealing with the Unexpected

Situations

1 You are entering a river which is about half a mile wide with rows of moorings along either bank. There is no wind and the main channel is too deep for anchoring. The engine stops suddenly and with a thump.

2 Leaving a busy river with quays on either bank and the engine begins running roughly. There is a fresh cross-wind.

3 The No Entry signal is hoisted just as you approach the entrance to the harbour. You are very low on diesel fuel and it may be a long wait. There is a lumpy sea running, a little tide flowing past the entrance and not much wind. It is a prohibited anchoring zone.

4 You have entered harbour and it is all strange to you. There is a yacht basin somewhere to port but that is all you know. Halfway along the approach channel a length of plastic wraps around your propeller and the engine stops. There is a light following breeze.

These situations are fairly run-of-the-mill emergencies. There is no risk to life but any one of them could land you in the sort of trouble that might prove expensive.

Plainly, the first requirement is to have a good working knowledge of your engine, to be familiar with the common causes of abrupt stoppage and general mechanical malingerings and how to deal with them. What is very important is to have some idea of how long it is likely to take to deal with the trouble. For instance, a two-stroke engine or outboard may tend to soot up the plug when slow running and to change the plug may take no longer than a minute. Or an engine may be subject to fuel starvation due to dirt in the tank and a blocked filter or jet. A case for more thorough maintenance perhaps, but not every owner is a paragon: it may be a ten-minute job. With a diesel, subject to air locks and the remedy a fiddly bleeding of the fuel line, perhaps longer than ten minutes and no guarantee of curing the fault first time.

Since in a family cruiser the skipper is also the navigator and the engineer, he will have to cope with the engine and handle or supervise the handling of the boat at the same time. He just cannot afford to be down below wrestling with a recalcitrant engine when he should be in full charge on deck. If he cannot say with certainty that he can fix the fault in a given time and if matters are becoming urgent up top, he must abandon the engine and seek an alternative.

What is always very surprising to a beginner is that there is almost always far more time than he expects before an immobile boat drifts into trouble. Needless to say, this excepts on-coming ships in narrow channels and fast tides or strong winds. In *average* conditions frenzied activity is scarcely ever required. Even in an emergency, when there is a need for fast work, a good seaman gives his whole attention to the job he is doing. One cannot do a quick plug change, for instance, while trying to keep an eye on the events taking place on deck. You can do one or the other. A plug dropped into the bilge exacerbates the situation. The questions to ask in this sort of emergency are 'How long have I got?' and 'Have I got long enough?' Thereafter, singlemindedness with an occasional look around to check that your time estimate was correct.

An engine that stops with a thump or any other foreign sound or symptom is usually going to stay stopped. In a tight spot the only justification for devoting time to a mysteriously defunct engine is when there is absolutely no other way of getting out of a jam. We are after all concerned with sailing craft. The next chapter deals with handling sails and later to handling the cruiser under sail alone, so we'll stick to our motor-or-drift theme for the time being.

It is tempting nowadays to invest a total trust in the auxiliary engine and it *should* be possible to do so. The hard truth is that few of us give as much attention to an auxiliary and its maintenance as we should; if we were really keen on engines we'd have a motor boat. From time to time our engines die on us. However easily remedied the fault, they just stop and whether the reason is a plastic bag wrapped around the propeller or a cooling water inlet choked or just a fuel stoppage, the fact remains that we should never be caught in a needlessly bad spot when it happens.

In Situation 2 where the engine is running roughly, the wise skipper first seeks the windward side of the channel and next orders some sail on her. By being on the windward side he has bought time should the engine stop altogether. In similar fashion a wise man never motors close to windward of any fixed object if he can avoid doing so – nor does he pass close up-stream of it. This is basic and right.

The predicaments in Situations 1, 3 and 4 above all call for an understanding of boat behaviour and drift characteristics. The boat in Situation 3 is faced with light-air sailing problems, but ultimately and when entering a strange yacht basin under sail the skipper will need to know how his boat will behave at slow speeds in order to know when to drop sails and carry her way into a vacant berth.

There is also a need to know how to judge distances over comparatively short ranges. How far away is the shore when the engine stops? How far ahead is that vacant berth? And so on. Almost always it is farther than you think. There are many methods of judging distance but every individual has his own built-in scale gleaned from experience. It is better to adopt one simple method and forget the rest. For instance, if with arm outstretched a man ashore is the same height as the nail of your little finger at 100 yards, that is all you may need much of the time. Get used to estimating your own boat length in multiples ahead. Standing at your tiller and staring forward, there will be a position on your mast, which might be the top of a cleat or a winch drum, and which when used as a sighting mark will carry your eye to a point on the water say two or three boat lengths ahead. It is worth experimenting to find what ranges you in your boat can fix on (Fig. 7).

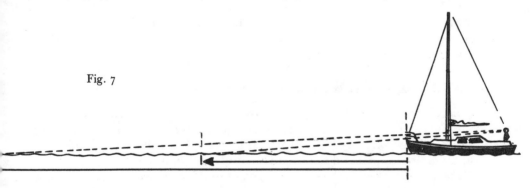

Fig. 7

A boat of average hull form and windage, allowed to drift, will usually take up a position with her bows turned downwind and at 45° to the wind direction. It varies a lot, though. If the tiller is lashed or just held to leeward she may head up until she is lying beam-on to the wind. This is the ideal angle for reducing the rate of drift, and one of the first actions in the event of an unheralded and unwanted engine stoppage will be to place the boat in her attitude of minimum drift.

A sailing cruiser with no sail set can also be 'sailed' to some degree under the windage of bare mast and rigging. Plainly she can be steered straight downwind, but she can also be made to sail at downwind angles of up to 30°–45°. Response to the helm will be slow and it will be necessary to begin a change of course well in advance. Also performance will vary greatly according to wind strength and hull profile, a boat with a good windward performance under sail being far more manoeuvrable under bare pole than one that makes a lot of leeway (Fig. 8).

In conditions of wind against tide or current a boat under bare pole can be very well under control, capable of being sheered across the current with the wind astern with such accuracy that the helmsman can put her

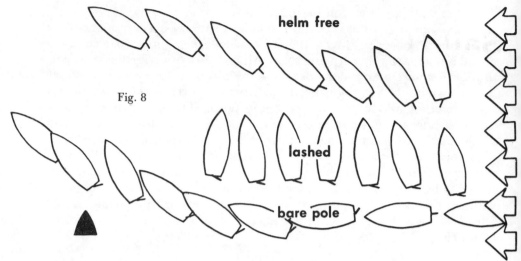

Fig. 8

almost exactly where he wants her to be. When the engine stops and you cannot anchor it needs very little breeze for her to be brought under at least partial control until sail can be set.

EXERCISE 1   Controlling drift rate

Find clear water and with all sail down switch off the engine and release the tiller. Note how the boat behaves and her final attitude of drift. Now lash the tiller hard over to leeward and see what attitude she adopts. Drop an anchored mark and note the rate and direction of drift away from it. Note the wind force at the time and carry out this exercise on other occasions in different weights of wind.

EXERCISE 2   Steering

Unlash the tiller and experiment. Let her come off before the wind and run her straight, letting speed build up. Try deviating to port and to starboard and note the maximum angle she will hold. Send crew to stand in the bows and see whether their windage alters your control. At maximum deviation, glance over the windward quarter and try to estimate the leeway.

EXERCISE 3   Distance judging

Whenever you are out walking and the opportunity occurs, note objects ahead such as typical two-storey buildings, people, cars, gates etc. Guess their distance and then count your paces. It is not merely size of distant objects but *detail* that gives the clue to distance. A window, for instance, loses its bars as distance increases, then its rectangular form, and finally it becomes a dot. Study the notes in the Appendix.

CHAPTER III
Sail Handling

Situations

1 You delayed reefing just a little too long and now, in a busy channel, it will have to be done in a hurry. Should you stay at the helm where you are most needed and let the job be done by people who are much slower, or would it be better to do it quickly and more neatly yourself?

2 You have the marina entrance half a mile ahead and you have a lot to do. How long dare you keep sail on her? The wind is dead astern and fresh.

3 With a fresh wind astern the mainsail is stowed hastily. Just as you reach the marina entrance it tears loose and begins to balloon out, obscuring your view.

4 A change down of headsails is needed. It is pretty rough and it is a dark night – not very safe up there on the foredeck, but a crew must learn. Have you trained them to tackle the job safely?

Before we can learn to handle a boat under sail in various weights of wind we have to become really competent in handling sails, in reefing and changing them at the right times and in delegating the job to crew.

A sail without wind to fill it is merely a sheet of canvas and it doesn't matter how large it is. From the moment a sail fills with wind it becomes a source of great power and a living force to contend with, controllable only by its sheets and by the handling of the boat. If it gets out of control it can be overpowering and the only way in which it can be tamed is by spilling the wind out of it. Often it is the helmsman who can tame a sail and throughout any sail changing or reefing operation he must keep an eye on proceedings. Every sail has its own particular problems.

THE MAINSAIL

A mainsail is hinged to the mast and wind is spilled by easing the sheet or luffing up. Provided it is a'shake it can be set or lowered with no trouble, but as soon as it begins to fill a bermudian sail binds hard against the track or spreaders and jams. A gaff mainsail can be set or lowered with the wind well aft, but it has its own special imp in the gaff which can slam to and fro in anything of a seaway and raise hell in its own right. A jammed mainsheet can sabotage either and a kink in the sheet can send a boat careering out of control with her mainsail only half set but filling prematurely. Any unnecessary emergency which causes people to begin rushing around on deck is hazardous – ask a trawlerman. Yet another mainsail problem is the tendency for a flogging sail to shed its leech battens. Good seamanship has its roots in little things like fixing a batten pocket if it isn't holding the batten firmly. The sight of a batten halfway out of its pocket sparks off a fine degree of panic and faces the skipper with a choice of losing control of the boat while the sail is lowered or losing the batten. I once lowered a mainsail for this reason just as the anchor was being brought in; the cruiser paid off with a half-set sail and I had to weave a wild course downwind through the moorings before I could find a clear space where I could round up and set the sail properly.

Reefing too has its snags. The hasty, badly made reef destroys the shape and power of the sail (Fig. 9). The smaller a sail is made by reefing the more important it becomes that it retains its driving efficiency because with the increasing pressure of the wind the slowing effect of hull and rigging windage rises. If the reduced sail also ceases to drive properly we are left with a labouring hulk that butts and bangs into the sea while making very little windward headway.

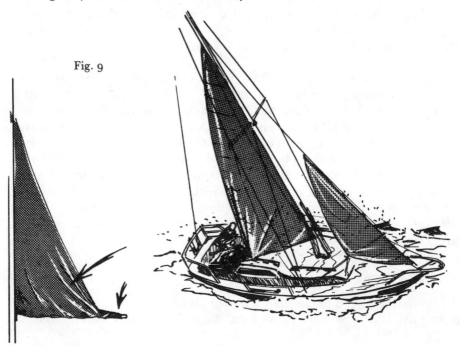

Fig. 9

A properly reefed mainsail has a taut luff, a clew which is pulled right out to its proper place, and a good curve to the draft of the sail between boom and luff with a taut leech. The slab reef or 'jiffy' reef is very much a favourite with the offshore racing fleets and it has largely taken over from roller reefing for several good reasons, mainly because a slab reef practically guarantees a good reef no matter how hurriedly it is put in.

The slab reef is really a development of the old points reefing system in which the reef is pulled down to the boom and the slack canvas tidied up later. The gooseneck has a hook to accommodate the new tack eye and there is a pendant to haul down the clew; thereafter the halyard is set up again and the sail is fully efficient. When there is time the slack canvas can be secured by means of hook and eye or whatever method, but the main job can often be done in well under a minute.

Roller reefing, on the other hand, is heir to a number of troubles. It can roll unevenly, producing a ghastly looking reef, or it can allow the end of the boom to droop (to the menace of the cockpit crew and the shame of all), or it can be just difficult to do quickly, which is bad news from any angle. The trouble is that it varies from boat to boat. In some cases one can roll in a good reef quickly and easily, first time and without any particular tricks, but in others a good reef is hard to achieve. All that can be said is that whatever system you own, you must regard it as one of the most important operations on board and learn to get the best from it – or chuck it out.

To reef a sail in harbour, head to wind, is no problem. However, it may be that the boat is in a marina berth and stern to wind so that the sail cannot be hoisted. A slab reef is easy enough but a rolled reef may be a bit tricky. The essential thing is to choose the first moment after leaving the berth to round up and set the sail, and decide whether the reef is good enough before the yacht leaves the shelter and gets to sea.

Reefing under way and probably in a squall is the true test of method. There is urgency, perhaps a good deal of violent motion and wind, also spray. The helmsman's part in the operation is as vital as that of those on the job. A racing crew expect to get very wet because the boat must be kept going, but a cruiser crew has no such pressure and the boat must be slowed right down to the point where she has bare steerage way, just enough to retain control at the helm. Either the sheets are eased right off and the yacht is allowed to lie athwart wind and sea, wallowing along, or she can be pointed up and the sheet eased just enough to take the power out of the sails. Some boats will lie very sweetly under headsail alone while the mainsail is half down. However it is done, though, it is the helmsman's job to watch the whole operation and provide as steady a platform as possible.

With roller gear it may vary from a simple matter of easing away the halyard with one hand while winding with the other, as the boom, supported by its topping lift, rolls up the sail without fuss. Other boats call for someone to haul the sail out aft along the boom as it turns. Where the sail is one of those which allows the boom end to droop, it may be necessary to lay some battens or a sailbag along the boom at the after end in order to build up the diameter there and prevent this. As a mainsail has a vertical luff and a leech which tapers from boom to masthead, when the boom is rotated the turns build up one over the other at the forward end but in a spiral at the after end – hence a thinner build-up and a drooping boom.

Hauling down a slab reef at sea is absurdly simple. It may vary a little but here is one sequence: sheet eased right off, clew pennant hauled down lifting the boom end, halyard lowered and tack eye hooked on, halyard set up again. Or the order may be reversed, taking the weight of the boom on the topping lift: sheet eased, halyard lowered and tack hooked on, clew hauled out and down and halyard set up again. The later tidying up of the loose sail along the boom can be delayed if it is urgent to get the boat under way again, or perhaps the after end is tidied up in order to leave the helmsman with an unrestricted view. The usual arrangement is a length of shockcord rove through a line of eyelets across the sail and put over corresponding hooks on the boom.

Lowering and stowing the mainsail is a job which is often left to novice members of the crew who have not been given any special instruction in the job. In nine cases out of ten they do it as a boat is heading upriver under motor and it is simple enough. Once berthed or moored the skipper tidies up the stow to his own liking. On the tenth occasion the wind is from astern and there is a lump of sea running: the job becomes difficult and very dangerous. The yacht is spun briefly head to wind while the sail is lowered, then put back on her course. At once the sail balloons up and becomes a wild animal, the yacht rolls mightily and the crew on the cabin top have their work cut out to hang on let alone get a good stow.

The essentials are: head to wind and sheet in hard against the topping lift as the sail rattles down. If the mainsheet has a cam cleat block for securing it, a wise skipper takes a quick hitch with the slack of the sheet as an additional safeguard because once the rolling begins, the crew at work will rely utterly on being able to hang on to the boom for support and if that mainsheet is freed by accident they will be straight overboard and hanging on to it. I had this done to me aboard a big ketch during an Irish Sea gale: I made three rapid trips across the deck, hanging on like grim death as I swept out over the water each time, and on the fourth trip dropped myself accurately on the miscreant who had let go the sheet. The crew must know how to muzzle the sail and get a tie round it before the yacht bears off and brings the wind aft again; then they can take their time.

Muzzling a wind-filled sail means first spilling the wind out of it. One method is to haul the leech forward and then grab hold of a big fold of sail along the boom and underneath the loose mass of sail above it. By pulling this (double) fold upwards it forms a sort of trough into which the loose canvas can be stuffed.

There are various sail ties to be bought. The one to watch is the short, doubled length of shockcord with the plastic bobble on one end (or both) which is secured around the sail by slipping the bobble through the eye on the other end. To my knowledge two people have had teeth knocked out by this gadget, and eyes have been damaged and even blinded when the ball snapped back under tension. The ordinary gasket – a 6ft strip of sailcloth or heavy webbing – takes some beating. It can be taken round the sail (middled) and the ends criss-crossed along the boom very quickly. Pending use, a gasket can be worn around the waist like a sash (Fig. 11).

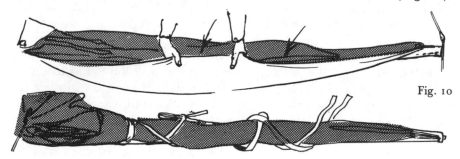

Fig. 10

HEADSAILS

Any headsail bent on but left lying unsecured at the foot of the stay will fill in any breeze and climb the stay. The foot may also blow through the lifelines and go overboard. Together these little mishaps can sabotage a tricky manoeuvre. Except for the odd occasion of motoring in a flat calm, no headsail should ever be left lying unsecured. Headsails are attached only to the forestay: consequently they are only half-captive and the second the sheet is eased they begin to flog. A flogging mainsail is captive between mast and boom but a headsail is free to lash as it pleases and in a hard breeze is capable of self-destruction and of making the foredeck a dangerous place to be. Thus in any headsail change, in strong conditions, it behoves the crew tending the sheets to let fly only when the person forward is ready to gather in the sail.

Headsails have enormous power and the change between a boat leaping and plunging to windward, hard on her ear and in a welter of spray, is dramatic when the headsail is handed. Getting rid of the headsail is usually the first step in taming an overpressed boat. Once down and unless a headsail change is planned the first task is to get a gasket or any sort of tier around sail and rail or pulpit, hauling the loose foot forward and securing the head down so that the sail can't go shimmying aloft again. At a pinch, a slack length of halyard can be passed around it and clove-hitched to the pulpit rail, but better still is to have a permanent length of shockcord seized to the pulpit for the purpose.

In a headsail change, then, the routine is something like this. New bag taken forward, sheets eased and halyard lowered, sail gathered in. Sail unhanked and sheets released, old sail down forehatch. New sail hanked on, sheets bent on, sail hoisted and halyard swigged, sheets hardened. Old sail bagged below and taken to its stowage. In addition, unclipping the tack and reclipping, readjustment of sheet leads, coiling the halyard and so on. Sailbags cannot be left lying on deck and must be hitched temporarily to the rail, winch handles have to be used and restowed. It can either be done systematically or it can be a lengthy mess.

For instance, time is saved by hanking on the new sail on a bare bit of stay below the old one and before touching either halyard or sheet. That way both sails are safe and it remains only to shift the tacks and halyard, unhank and shift the sheets. Speed isn't always important but safety is always so. Now and again, though, a fast headsail change may be essential. A crew that has been taught can move fast and be efficient, but if they haven't been taught the job any attempt at speed becomes hazardous.

The things that go wrong in a fast headsail change are: losing the halyard (either end) which streams to leeward out of reach, losing a big bight of sail overboard, losing a sailbag or a winch handle and slipping or tripping. At night slack halyard can take a turn around the spreaders and serious damage can result when the sail is hoisted and winched taut. By securing the tails of all halyards and by insisting that crew hitch or clip the halyard to the rail, that they know better than to stand on wet sailcloth or get to leeward of a sail, and that they work to a system most of these troubles can be eliminated.

A modern genoa can be considerably larger than a mainsail and for a small family crew it can be a formidable thing to handle. With a weak crew the rule should be to change down before you *have* to. When the first doubt enters your mind, when you remark that 'We'll have to think about changing down soon', *that* is the time to do it.

The advent of sophisticated roller headsails has brought a totally new dimension to cruising under sail. Expensive though these may be they are an absolute boon. One must accept that an all-purpose genoa is less efficient half-rolled than a smaller headsail would be, but only marginally so. The real gain is that the boat always has the right sail forward for the conditions. When one might think twice about changing back to a smaller sail ten minutes after changing up again, with a roller gear one does it automatically. The simple matter of easing the sheet and winding a winch handle is no trouble and it is done from the dry safety of the cockpit. The sheet lead position *should* be shifted for each alteration in sail area, but in practice one lead position covers about a third of the range of sail reductions, hence about three possible lead positions are used. Since the sail reduction needed most often will be the reduction from full to one-third rolled, shifting the lead doesn't happen too frequently.

MAST-STOWING MAINSAILS

The mast-stowing mainsail, pioneered in America, is fast gaining popularity. Like the roller headsail these mainsails have a rotating stay, but it is inside the mast which is a specially designed spar of larger cross-section and with a track of a width and shape to allow the sail to be drawn through it easily. The sail also is of special design and necessarily battenless. The stay is rotated by a drum and furling line and the operation is simple and, with ordinary care to keep a little tension on it, fault-free. The system makes it easy to reduce sail without leaving the cockpit and combined with a roller headsail the rig becomes as near to effortless sail handling as one could imagine. A variation of the rolled mainsail has an exterior roller and a standard mast can be adapted – it is in fact a roller headsail arrangement set vertically close abaft the mast. It is said to be effective, but perhaps there is more room for snags to develop by comparison with the inside-mast arrangement, which is stressed in column, i.e. in line with the mast rather than *outside* it.

SPINNAKERS

If you have a crew which is nervous of a spinnaker in anything above a light breeze, it is best to leave it in its bag or embark on a deliberate training session. Unlike the other sails aboard, a spinnaker has all the ingredients for a panic of regal proportions. Unlike the others, it is controlled only by its corners. It flies like a kite. It is docile as long as it is asleep. The moment it is allowed to flog it takes over the ship. There are clever tube devices that make spinnaker setting and dousing comparatively simple, but it is important to know how to handle the sail conventionally, setting it from the turtle bag in the pulpit and handing it by letting fly the tack and hauling it in under the lee of the mainsail.

The particular gremlins in the spinnaker are premature filling when half hoisted, wineglassing around the forestay, snagging on the leeward spreaders, skying high above the mast on a runaway halyard, falling in the water under the bows, and twisting. Then there is the risk of a broach in too much wind, the chance of the pole taking charge and rising vertically, and several other charming tricks. To use a spinnaker properly, driving a boat to her maximum speed, a skipper must either decide to study it and train a crew or leave it home in the airing cupboard.

Under spinnaker a boat is only half under command, that is to say she can only be sailed downwind or on a broad reach; she cannot be taken anywhere near the wind or deviated downwind without a tricky gybing operation. Therefore, one of the most vital of all spinnaker operations is to be able to get it down, off the deck and a headsail back in its place. Remember, one cannot even motor back to windward with a spinnaker still set: it must come down – fast. What a skilled racing crew can do is one thing, and a small cruising crew yet another.

CRUISER CHUTES

The 'cruiser chute' is an attempt to give the cruising man a compromise. This new big sail is intended to give sail area off the wind without the complexities of a spinnaker. In fact it is really no compromise, because being set flying (not hanked to a stay) it shares the same wayward characteristics as a spinnaker without being as efficient, either as a running or a reaching sail. Intended for light airs and up to maybe Force 3, it can be the devil's own job to handle in anything above that weight of wind – desperate in a sudden squall.

Perhaps it is unfair to be so sweepingly damning because there are many versions of the basic idea and each maker has a different approach. Some chutes are designed to float high, others to have the luff set up tight; some go for sheer size, others for ease of handling and so forth; but apart from the 'floaters' (and it is usually better to take down the mainsail altogether if the wind is dead astern) a maximum area lightweight ghoster genoa that can be boomed out for running is probably a more useful and certainly a more easily handled sail.

STOWING

Mainsail stowing was touched on earlier. The aim should be to form an outer skin by hauling up that double fold from underneath and shaking the loose sail down into it. I see no credit whatsoever in making an untidy stow, however secure the sail may be. One has to have that small edge of pride. With gaff rig a mainsail stow can be beautifully neat, but an awful lot of people with bermudian mainsails are content to get the cover on and hide the mess underneath.

Headsail stows are temporary. When you finish sailing the sail must be bagged and sent below. On the other hand there is sound sense in leaving a

Fig. 11

working jib hanked on if there is some chance that it may be needed in a hurry. Engine reliability we have commented on. It much depends whether you have spent a lifetime sailing dear old clumbungays with engines like a bucket of conjuring tricks (as I have prior to the latter years), or whether you have never known other than utter reliability.

A headsail stow, then, must keep it off the deck and clear of muddy anchor work while leaving it ready for quick setting. My own answer is to leave it hanked on with the tack still fast and only the halyard and the sheets detached. The whole sail can then be bundled into its sailbag, which is drawn taut, the sheets are hitched high up the forestay and set up taut, and the halyard is hanked to the pulpit and tightened. With a clip shackle on the halyard and either two bowlines to make for the sheets or a toggle (Fig. 11) it takes perhaps half a minute to have the sail ready to hoist.

IN GALE FORCE WINDS

The whole conception of handling sails alters dramatically when the wind rises. In a fresh breeze, Force 5, sail handling is difficult enough. There will be lively motion, wet and slippery decks, lashing sheets and flogging sails. A full gale is almost double the strength of a fresh breeze. No matter how skilful the helmsman, the yacht will be laid hard over, plunging and rolling, and sails thunder and crack, hammering the working crew, wrenching free of their grasp and possessing a frightening energy. In these conditions sails must not be allowed to flog any more than is unavoidable. Not only do they shake the whole rig, loosening anything not absolutely secure, but they are self-destructing. In the days of cotton sails only those in perfect condition could stand this violence : others disintegrated within seconds. Today's synthetic fibre canvas can take tremendous punishment, but it needs only one small weakness or a seam with a few chafed stitches for a sail to begin to come apart. In a gale it may be highly dangerous to lose an important sail.

Sail changes, then, must be planned very carefully. The sail must be got off fast and stowed with double care. Likewise the new sail or the reefed mainsail must go up quickly and be sheeted in the instant it is taut in the luff. It is vital, though, that it is set correctly. Sails are often set hurriedly and badly in gale conditions, with dire consequences later.

Sail handling in high winds means close teamwork, full use of safety harness, scrupulous care not to get to leeward of a sail and someone to control the sheets. Headsail sheets allowed full freedom to flog will take three turns around everything in the batting of an eye. Halyard tails, too. In fact, rope care at all times is an essential part of the seaman's skill. The first thing that happens in any hectic sailing situation is the snarling up of ropes – the second thing that happens is that a sheet won't run or a halyard gets foul aloft, then the band really does begin to play.

EXERCISE 1   On the mooring or in the berth: reefing

Experiment to see how deeply the mainsail can be reefed, either by roller or slab reefing. Unless the sail can be reduced to one-third of its full area and retain an efficient shape it cannot be regarded as controllable or suitable for gale conditions at sea. Set the storm jib and check that the sheet lead is correct.

EXERCISE 2   Crew drill

Make a point of watching your crew at work without their being aware of it. Time them in a sail change or in reefing. Notice how many unecessary stages are included. Without appearing to be an impossible fusspot, introduce a few changes. Do the jobs yourself as often as possible. Take the boat out singlehanded and carry out these jobs – it is the surest way of finding out where improvements can be made and in learning not to holler at your crew.

EXERCISE 3   Spinnaker

If you are inexperienced in spinnaker handling, stow your pride and ask an experienced racing man to come out with you. Resolve not to use it until your crew is fully competent and at ease in handling it. Practice handing and stowing. It is too costly to learn a spinnaker by trial and error.

CHAPTER IV
Handling Under Sail

Situations

1 Force 5 and a choppy sea. A sailing dinghy capsizes nearby and you are the only boat available to help an obviously novice helmsman and crew. It will have to be done under sail because your engine is out of order – but how?

2 Running with a smart breeze, everybody relaxed and happy. Suddenly it's 'Man overboard!' and everybody is shouting at once. What should you do?

3 Tacking fast among densely moored craft. While spinning her around in a tight gap the jib sheet suddenly fouls up on a mast cleat: there's no room to have a second try. What now?

The modern sailing cruiser is a miracle of handiness compared to her older long-keeled sisters. The rig is simple and the performance is nimble and it should be possible to manoeuvre such a boat into almost any corner, provided she can be handled at slow speed but under absolute control.

Spilling and filling is the basis. Spilling wind by easing sheets or luffing to slow the boat, and filling the sails by hardening sheets or bearing away to regain power and drive. There is a minimum speed for every boat at which full control can be kept and below which she becomes sluggish and uncertain to control. It is more important to be able to handle a boat at slow speeds and with confidence than it is to be able to chuck her around at dizzy speed. With time one can learn how to sail fast right up to the point of manoeuvre and then stop her, retaining just the right speed for the purpose.

At slow speeds every boat has her stalling point. With some, as steerage way is lost the headsail begins to dominate, forcing the bows off to leeward and requiring more rudder, which further slows her unless speed can be increased quickly. There is also a big difference between slow speed manoeuvres in light airs and those in a fresh breeze, where the boat has to be slowed down by freeing sheets or holding her a'quiver, close into the wind. With the former, the helmsman is intent on getting all he can out of a meagre breeze, consistent with the speed he needs. With the latter there is windage to contend with. As speed is lost by spilling wind the wind pressure on hull and rigging begins to affect steering. Quite often you will see a boat progressing in a series of jerks, first heeled hard over as she regains lost way, then coming up all a'shake as the helmsman tries to counter the sudden spurt ahead. A sudden squall can stop a boat dead in her tracks and all control is lost.

A helmsman can either jerk his headsail up to weather in order to make the bows pay off, thereby collecting wind in his main and restoring drive, or he can let the boat begin to move astern, then reverse his rudder blade so that the stern is canted to port when he wants the bows to pay off to starboard and vice versa. At slow speeds a sailing boat is like a see-saw; first the mainsail drives her bow up into the wind, then the headsail forces it off again: the helmsman plays with sails and rudder the whole time. If he is trying to tack and he has lost too much way – perhaps there is a slight sea – he hardens the mainsheet and lets fly the jib until, having passed the eye of the wind, he can hold it a'back to help turn her. Or he wants to bear away in a tight downwind turn. Now he lets fly the mainsheet completely and hauls his jib a'back simultaneously with forcing the helm over.

Finding this optimum slow handling speed is the first job we must tackle in learning a particular boat and the end of chapter exercises are designed to do this. We must also consider the effect of the *apparent* wind, though.

We can't learn to sail without becoming well aware of the difference between true and apparent wind. A boat lying stopped with the wind on her beam, sails shaking, feels a true wind. As sheets are hardened and the boat begins to move, her own speed combines with the true wind speed to produce an apparent wind which is now no longer dead on her beam but some way forward of it. As speed increases it moves even farther forward until a really fast boat will be sailing almost closehauled.

In terms of slow speed manoeuvres, it also means that an approach to a mooring buoy with a beam (true) wind in which the helmsman is relying on being able to ease the sails right off in order to slow down and finally stop doesn't work out that way. He eases sheets right off: the headsail is free to flog but the mainsail cannot be eased off far enough because of the after shrouds and as the speed falls and the apparent wind creeps aft the time comes when only by bearing off and then luffing up, or by dropping the mainsail can he shake the wind out of it.

A similar thing happens when we luff for a buoy in a fresh breeze. We *think* we are dead to leeward of it and luff hard, but as the boat slows we find that the true wind is in fact still filling the sails and so we have to ease sheets as well as luffing head to wind. The safest approach is on a close reach: the sheets can be used like throttle levers, easing to slow her,

hardening to give her more speed, and finally letting them go completely
(Fig. 12).

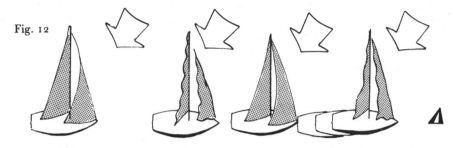

Fig. 12

In our three situations above we had two cases requiring slow speed
control and one calling for a fast turn downwind. Taking this one first it is
interesting to note how reluctant people are to exploit the tight downwind
turning ability of most boats. The temptation to try another tack, although
instinct tells them that there isn't enough way on the boat to get her
through the wind, is almost irresistable. A missed tack, the boat losing
steerage, bearing off and careering into the nearest hard object is a
familiar denouement. Bearing off, unless you know your boat's turning
circle for that weight of wind, can be a bit hair-raising. She gathers speed
alarmingly and *before* life comes back into the tiller, therefore you feel out
of control. But with the mainsail *right* off (and this means helping the
sheet to run) and the jib backed hard a boat sits back on her rudder blade
and spins. In Situation 3 our man might well have employed this tactic to
get out of his mess.

We will be dealing at length with Man Overboard later on, so we'll look
at Situation 1 in which the crew of a capsized dinghy must be rescued. The
first need is to get people out of the water (dealt with in Man Overboard
later) but it is the handling of the boat that concerns us now.

A first approach run might be made for the dual purpose of giving
confidence to people in the water (ideally this would be on a reaching
course for reasons discussed above and because speed can be controlled),
also to give our skipper time to think out his plan. Assuming no close and
dangerous lee shore, he will probably return on the opposite reach,
slowing but keeping control and aiming to stop to leeward of the capsized
boat. It must be exactly right. Too far from her and survivors will have
to let go of their safe hold to reach the yacht and too close might mean
crushing them (as would certainly happen if he went to windward of
them).

Very likely, although one cannot be dogmatic, the best plan would be
to get a line on the dinghy and at *once* drop the cruiser's sails. She can then
ride to the dinghy like a sea-anchor while the survivors are helped aboard.
Or, if the water is shallow enough, the cruiser crew can lay hold of the
dinghy and then drop anchor and sails instantly. I rescued a man and girl

catamaran crew in this way. It was very rough and I knew that it would be all my wife and I could do to handle the cruiser let alone help exhausted people on board. I secured to the cat by throwing a dinghy anchor through her rigging. Whatever the method, it depends on expert fast sail handling and rope handling. One thing is certain: in any breeze no cruiser is going to be easy to handle unless she can either be shorn of sail or allowed to lie-to, or heave-to, so that the helm can be left and headway is taken off.

HEAVING-TO AND LYING-TO

Wind direction is the baseline for all sailing manoeuvres. While the wind is ahead of the beam a boat can be stopped by luffing and freeing sheets. When it comes abaft the beam the only way to stop or slow her is to take the sails down. We must also hark back to that basic tendency of almost all boats to stick their tails upwind as soon as they lose steerage way – thereby filling their sails and probably luffing themselves, repeating the whole switchback manoeuvre over and over again.

Heaving-to consists of bringing the boat closehauled, then hauling the clew of the jib across the deck to windward, while leaving the mainsail sheeted. The rudder is then turned, lashing the tiller down to leeward, to produce an into-wind turning force. There will be very little forward way and so the rudder merely holds the bows up against the leeward-turning thrust of the backed jib.

In actual fact, and with modern boats, it doesn't always work out quite like that. Pinned hard in, a boat begins to swoop and curve, luffing and paying off alternately, or even going round in circles. Usually it is best to

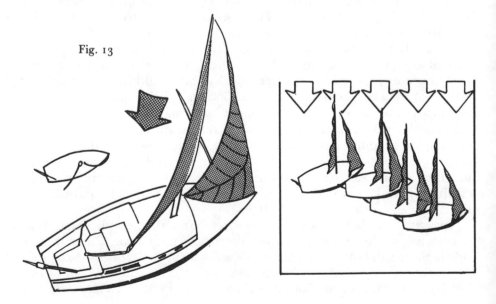

Fig. 13

slow right down first, then haul the jib to weather until the clew is exactly on the mast. The mainsail is paid off until it lies at about 45° to the fore-and-aft line and then, with helm lashed, she should lie a'shake and quite quietly (Fig. 13). Lying-to is a variant. It consists of allowing the boat to lie broadside to the wind with both sails completely free and shaking, helm lashed a'lee. Consequently, while a boat could lie properly hove-to under a storm jib and deeply reefed mainsail, or even main only (or in some cases jib only) and not do worse than an occasional flogging of sails, one would not lie-to in the manner I have described in anything more than a light breeze. Or perhaps temporarily in an emergency when the flogging sails have to be ignored in the interest of stopping the boat for a particular and urgent reason – such as our dinghy rescue (Fig. 13 inset).

The value of stopping a boat at sea, of winning breathing space to get ready for entering harbour, to sort out a puzzling navigational situation, or just to enjoy the respite or to have a meal in peace, cannot be over-stressed. Few people do it. The natural tendency is to sail flat out the whole time.

EXERCISE 1   Slow speed handling

Put the boat on a close reach and ease sheets until the sails are shaking, allow the boat speed to fall until you have barely steerage way. Now harden the mainsail just enough to send it to sleep. In a moderate to fresh breeze this will be more than enough to restore good steerage way without touching the jib. According to the strength of the wind, experiment until you have found the sheet setting that gives the minimum control necessary for tacking. Now put her hard on the wind and continue to experiment. From time to time stop her completely by easing both sheets. Notice her behaviour while losing steerage way and whether she pays off downwind.

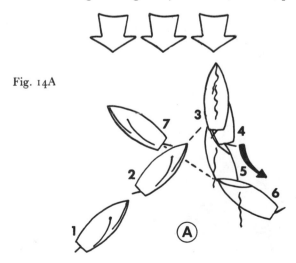

Fig. 14A

Exercise 2   Use of the sternboard (Fig. 14A)

Bring her slowly up into the wind losing way gradually and let the jib
sheets fly. When all headway is lost watch what she does. She may simply
fall off away from the wind, whereupon the mainsail will fill and she will
drive ahead. Or she may fall astern. If this happens try to make her pay
off on the tack you choose. If you want her bows to fall off to port the rudder
blade must be put to starboard. Repeat this exercise, stopping dead then
trying to back her round on her rudder without the help of the backed jib;
keep at it until you can be sure of paying off on the tack you have chosen.

EXERCISE 3   Paying off and wearing round (Fig. 14B)

Stop her head to wind again. This time back the jib to port and free the
mainsheet off completely. Put the rudder to port. (*Note:* I designate
rudder instead of helm or tiller because some readers may have wheel
steering.) The boat will sit back on her rudder and pay off quickly to
starboard. Give her full starboard rudder as she brings the wind abeam
and let her go right round and through a gybe. With the mainsheet
hardened in for the gybe let it take her round full circle to closehauled
again.

Sail closehauled to build up good steerage way, then bear away on full
rudder but without easing the mainsheet and note what sort of turning
circle she makes before she brings the wind dead astern. (This manoeuvre
may prove difficult in a fresh breeze and is best tried in a moderate wind.)
Now repeat the manoeuvre, this time freeing the mainsheet as in the
previous exercise.

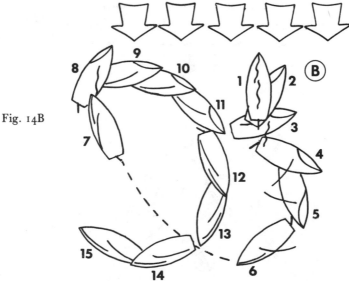

Fig. 14B

EXERCISE 4   Catherine wheel (Fig. 15A)

This exercise is really for fun but it does give a good indication of boat balance. Quite simply, come up into the wind with sails close but not tightly sheeted, and tack. Keep the helm where it is, full over, so that the boat goes through stays and continues to bear away, then gybes and spins up into the wind to tack again, and so on. With the helm lashed and in a moderate wind most modern boats will continue to tack, gybe, tack, gybe for as long as you care to leave them. Children love this exercise, which is a good enough reason to carry it out.

Fig. 15A

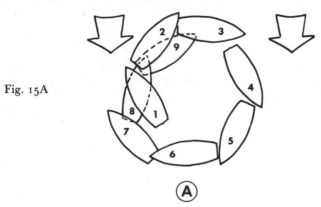

EXERCISE 5   Sailing a box

Drop your drift mark. Start off by getting to leeward of it, then try to sail a box pattern with the mark in the centre. Closehauled, run with wind on the quarter, gybe and bring the wind on the other quarter, complete with another closehauled leg (Fig. 15B). The aim is to make the box smaller and smaller. In a fresh breeze the sheet handlers will be working like clockwork

Fig. 15B

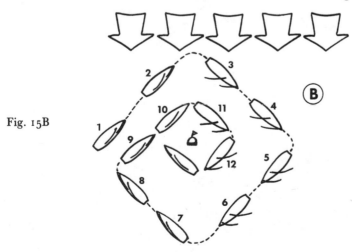

hens, so be merciful. This is a splendid quickening-up exercise though. The box pattern gives you a purpose for handling the boat. It can also be tried under mainsail only and under headsail only.

EXERCISE 6   Luffing for the mark

Anchor the drift mark. The simple aim is to bring up head to wind on the mark. Make the first run on a broad reach gauged so that you can luff at it from a couple of boat lengths to leeward. You may need half a dozen shots from both directions before you begin to judge the wind direction correctly – and remember your true/apparent wind allowance. Now try a close-hauled approach, this time luffing from about a length to leeward. It will of course much depend on wind strength how far you'll need to shoot for it. Next try a dead run, passing the mark a length away on the beam (or further according to wind strength) and luffing full round. This is very difficult to judge and rarely a manoeuvre to try in anger. Lastly, make the close-reach approach, playing the sheets as you go to adjust speed (Fig. 16).

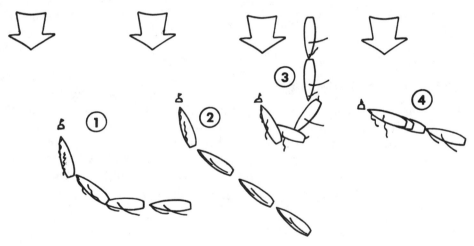

Fig. 16

CHAPTER V

Handling in Yacht Harbours

Situations

1 A fresh breeze is holding the yacht pinned against the berth jetty and you cannot get clear.

2 Just as you are entering the approach lane to your marina berth a stranger pips you to it. There is a stiff following breeze and there are no other empty berths to be had. He can't hear you yelling. There is another yacht close astern.

3 There is a vacant berth astern of you and a stranger is coming in. He looks to be taking it far too fast. He is about four lengths away: what should you do?

It is an ironic fact of life that many total beginners take delivery of their new boats in a marina berth. What little experience they will have had has probably been under the eye of an instructor or certainly in easier conditions. It is easy enough to motor clear of the marina on a calm day, far less easy to enter and berth again later. If the breeze has piped up by then the startled skipper may be facing a task that would tax an experienced hand.

A whole lot of trouble can be avoided by taking time to think things out in advance. Prior to leaving, a skipper should sniff at the breeze, gauging its direction, strength and tendency – is it a bit squally? He can plan his engine manoeuvres. If he has been able to work through the preceding exercises he will have a good idea what he can do with the boat. If he is starting in raw, he should most certainly have invited a more experienced friend along.

He should do his own thinking, though. Wind, tidal current if any, the movements of other craft, the order of letting go warps, and what is more important, a moment or so foreseeing what might possibly go wrong.

The same rules apply to the return. The instinct is to aim for the entrance and go for it bald-headed. Unless it is obviously quite a simple approach it does no harm to throttle right down to a tickover and study the problem, while the crew is readying the fenders and lines. He should by now know how his boat lies when way is off her, or he can motor in a gentle circle to size things up. He can then go in slowly at what he will know to be the minimum speed while retaining full control. Every harbour or marina looks small and congested from outside and usually one is surprised to find upon entering that there is a good deal more room than there seemed – occasionally, though, they *are* small and congested. Thus the value of this caution and time spent sniffing around outside before tackling a strange port.

Once inside, making for the berth and with crew standing ready, a skipper is concerned with stopping the boat. His crew should in fact be sitting rather than standing, or at any rate out of his line of sight. In order to gauge the speed of the boat it is as important to be able to see on either side and astern and all too often a nervous skipper begins to natter and nag simply because he has that hemmed-in feeling.

The manoeuvres and exercises in Chapter 1 on handling under power should have prepared him for berthing, for using the side-paddle effect going astern (or being prepared to counter it if it is going to swing his stern out of rather than into the berth) and for judging wind effect. His first task is to bring the boat close enough and slowly enough to the jetty or catwalk for one of his crew to *step* ashore. That they should be able to step and not have to leap ashore is highly important. It is far better to make a clumsy but very gentle approach which allows someone to get ashore with a line than it is to go swiping in like a cavalry charge howling 'JUMP for God's sake!' Invariably there will be some brave idiot who will try it, but a chunk out of your bow is a temporary injury and a stunned and then drowned man is for keeps.

Getting a line ashore means two things. With a line fast to a bollard astern the remaining headway can be checked smoothly and with a line from the right end of the boat her possible tendency to swing outwards can be thwarted. This means having a good hand ashore and one who is as much aware of what has to be done as is the skipper.

Ordinarily there will be two lines aboard and ready to use, one forward and the other one aft. In normal procedure the bow line end will be secured to the foredeck, led out through the bow fairlead and aft again, outside everything. The usual place from which a crew will step out onto the jetty is just by the fore rigging, thus he can hang on to the shrouds for balance while he stands outside the rail ready to go. If the skipper has made a real hash of things he may have to take off from outside the bow pulpit, but it isn't advisable and he will certainly have to jump.

He will run aft on the jetty and catch a turn around any cleat or bollard he can find, then surge his warp bringing the yacht to a standstill. The skipper may give a touch astern, but if this means throwing his stern outwards from the jetty it may be a light one. With a breeze blowing *out* of the berth there will be no time to lose now. Having stopped the yacht the skipper will be stepping ashore with the stern line (or directing somebody else to do so) while our first hand is taking his rope forward to another bollard to hold the bows in. Neatly done and no fuss, but it could have gone wrong if the line work had been muffed (Fig. 17A).

Watch her come in again. This time it is the stern line which is taken ashore; the crew has to nip back along the jetty to find a bollard suitably far astern for stopping purposes and having found one and caught a turn he brings her up all right, but that offshore breeze instantly takes the bows downwind and she ends up moored by her tail. Or suppose he took the bow line correctly and stopped her correctly but muffed the stern line (or the skipper did): away goes her stern and now she ends up moored by her bow (Fig. 17B and C).

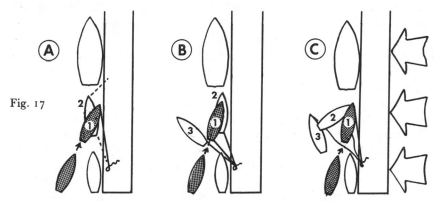

Fig. 17

People handling ropes should know what is expected of them and what the yacht is likely to do. A new owner with a novice crew cannot expect to stay safe from bumps and bangs unless and until he trains his crew. An hour or so just sitting and watching in any busy yacht harbour on a Sunday evening as the weekenders are returning is a valuable experience. You will see every sort of handling from the completely expert – which will be so incident-free that you may not even notice a boat come in – to the spectacularly incompetent; each has as much to teach as the other.

HANDLING ROPES

One usually handles a boat into her berth on the lines which are to be used for mooring, but if these are by some chance heavy and stiff or of that slippery, springy polypropylene stuff it is far better to choose light nylon or Terylene (Dacron) lines, strong enough to check her on but light enough to handle easily. This also means suitable for throwing because there is often a bystander who will take a line for you. Wherein lies a hidden peril. There is absolutely no guarantee that he knows what in hell to do with your line having caught hold of it. Foredeck crew must be ready and able to put a rapid bowline in the end before heaving it and to tell the shore helper exactly which bollard it should be dropped over.

A line for throwing is best coiled small, split into a larger and a smaller coil and either one of these thrown, according to distance. Half a boat's length is about the maximum safe distance for anybody not expert at it and the shorter the distance the better. The aim is to land a good solid lump of the coil on the target; the bare end may land but not one recipient in five will be quick enough to grab it. If he or the line misses there isn't much time left: the yacht is still moving ahead. However little time is left, though, the line heaver *must re-coil carefully*. A muffed first shot followed by another failure due to a hastily coiled line is so familiar – and so is the crunch which follows.

A coiled line laid on deck cannot be expected to run cleanly. Thus our man ashore with the other end trying to haul in the slack may find that the coil jams and he hasn't enough line left for taking a proper turn. If a line is to run unattended it must not be coiled, it must be flaked down. This simply means dropping the rope on deck in an *apparent* tangle, each turn lying across the one below, just as it falls from the hands. Provided it is not disturbed it will run clean.

The common faults in handling berthing lines are failure to coil and throw correctly, slowness in making a bowline, failure to take a line outside all rails and rigging, the skipper's failure to make clear his plan of action, getting lines hung up under the fenders ranged along the topsides, failure of a rope to run cleanly off the coil, lines supposedly made fast to a deck cleat which come adrift and of course slowness in anything. It is one of the anomalies of sailing that a vehicle so slow in real speed terms as a small boat should demand such speed and dexterity of her crew.

WARPING

A yacht in her berth is not always easily got out of it. The wind can be pinning her against the catwalk, as in Situation 1. In moderate winds her bow or stern can be poled out with the boathook allowing the engine to pull or push her out. She will have to go straight out and in a straight line, until bow or stern, as the case may be, are clear of the bows or sterns of craft in berths next to her. Any use of the rudder will cause the opposite end of the yacht to swing in and clout them, which prevents her from turning (Fig. 18A).

In stronger winds this method won't work. The boat will blow back into the berth, boathooks or not, unless her bow or stern can be forced out against the wind by at least 30°–45°. It may be possible to *spring* her out. A line from the bow is led aft to the catwalk about halfway along her length and then the engine is put slow ahead until she is leaning against the spring, bows against the catwalk fendering. With the rudder hard over towards the catwalk engine revs are increased smoothly and her stern will begin to spring outwards. Aided by boathooks and maybe the spinnaker pole, it should be possible to reach the required angle. The engine is shifted smoothly but quickly to full astern and the bow spring is slipped (Fig. 18B).

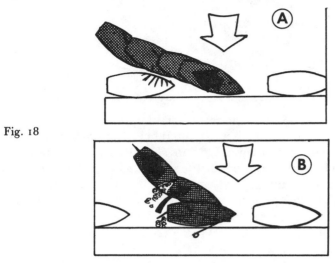

Fig. 18

A word on slipping a line. It will have been doubled back to the deck after passing through a ring ashore or around a bollard or cleat. The lazy end to be slipped *must* have a tightly whipped snag-free bitter end, and it must be drawn free with care, never, *never* snatched or jerked, or the bitter end may flick itself into a hitch around any nearby projection or the cleat itself. Should this happen, let the whole line go. Never attempt to heave at it, which might well cant the bows around and ruin the manoeuvre.

Getting into a downwind berth is even more difficult in a fresh breeze. Any attempt to place the yacht beam-on in a limited space calls for great skill. Knowing the power of your engine astern is the secret, also how it will deflect her stern (side-paddle effect ASP: astern-stern-to-port with a right-handed screw). A skilled handler will bring up off his berth a half length to windward and let her blow in (Fig. 19A). Even so she may

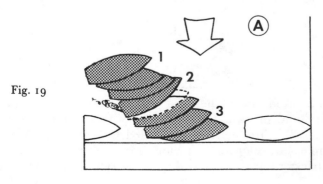

Fig. 19

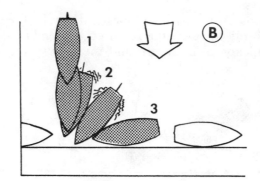

Fig. 19B

instantly swing her bows in with a crash. Berthing port side to, the engine going astern will help straighten her up, but if berthing starboard side to it may swing her stern further upwind. One possible albeit clumsy manoeuvre is to go straight in bow first, aiming for the starboard end of the berth, and hold her off with a powerful burst astern just before the bow gets too close. With a marked side-paddle effect the stern will then cant to port and allow the yacht to fall into her berth correctly (Fig. 19B).

Failing the earlier methods of leaving a leeward berth, there remain hauling off by means of a line carried right across the marina lane, liable to win a skipper much vilification from other owners bent on avoiding it, or asking the harbour launch to tow him out. If the yacht is berthed on the end of a finger pier it may also be easy to warp her to leeward around the end of it (Fig. 20A).

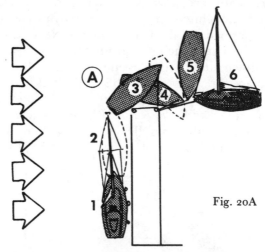

Fig. 20A

Another familiar situation is when the yacht lies in a berth which lies up and down wind and she is facing the wrong way for an easy exit. She must then be *winded* (pronounced 'wynded'). This end-for-ending procedure is simple, but bugged by a hidden snare if the wind is strong (Fig. 20B). The tricky moment arises when halfway through the turn and

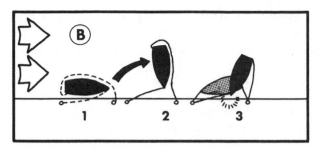

Fig. 20B

bow or stern, whichever is downwind, suddenly drives into the catwalk, hard. The hand who has line B in the sketch must not begin to heave on it until the boat has passed the midway point: then he must heave hard and get in all the slack he can before taking a turn to hold her.

In Situations 2 and 3 we tackle a very different aspect of close water boat handling, the matter of custom and usage. To be beaten to your own berth by a total stranger and do nothing about it seems to call for saintly qualities, but really it is a matter of getting priorities right. Just about all such situations do. Your first call is the safe handling of the boat and the boat astern. Your berth must wait. Once you can extricate yourself by judicious signalling and manoeuvring, you can drop alongside some other boat temporarily and walk round to the transgressor and put him straight. The alternative, to pursue him, hollering, could mean that the stranger would have backed out athwart your heading and so might begin a memorable pile-up.

Situation 2 is tricky. The strange skipper may be highly expert and in complete charge – or he may be on the threshold of a new and expensive discovery. You must not start yelling. It is a curious thing, but the observer can often be in a better position to judge how a vessel will behave and how she should be handled than the helmsman. On the other hand he knows (or should know) what his own boat will do in a given set of circumstances. The only reasonable course in this case would be to leap ashore and let go your own stern line, telling your crew to fend the stern out while you gesture to the newcomer that you are ready for his line. At a pinch and if she really can't stop soon enough, her bows can slip between your stern and the catwalk with minimum damage to you. What you have really done, though, is to imply urgency and emergency without angering an already tense skipper.

In tricky marina situations keep the temperature down, think ahead, and remember your spreaders and those of the other boats. Remember too that damaged boats are better than damaged people.

The finger-pier layout of most marinas is designed to provide maximum berthing with reasonably good access. In some cases, though, good approach lanes are sacrificed in order to cram in a few more berths. In the usual layout there are the main pontoon arms with the fingers at right angles like fish bones. This means that all approaches to berths involve a final right-angle turn to enter and bring up alongside a finger.

A head to wind berth entry is straightforward enough. A strong following breeze is tricky if going full astern means throwing her tail to port in a starboard side berth, but simpler otherwise. When the wind is across or aslant the berth there can be problems following the final right angle turn. Once a boat begins swinging in such a sharp turn it isn't always easy to steady her up in the short distance remaining and over-correction of the helm can mean loss of control at slow speeds.

Given a cross-wind the final length or so to the berth alongside can become a nightmare if the helmsman loses control. He will probably resort to bursts ahead and astern in an attempt to straighten her up – rarely successful – and the odds are that he will end up with his boat stuck athwart the sterns of other moored craft. The most sensible course is to pull astern, right out of the berth, and having turned round in open water make a completely fresh approach. The essence of the thing is that if one has the skill and confidence (and the braking power going astern) to come in boldly and carrying good way, if one can motor confidently straight into the berth and then stop her dead, most of the problems are overcome. It is the very slow, very timid approach that messes things up. Ironically, little damage is done by being timid and one hell of a lot can be done by unskilled boldness.

In early days there is a lot to be said for swallowing the pride and going in on a slant and then manhandling her in (Fig. 21). Boat A is to leeward of the finger and she puts her bow in, allowing the crew to land and/or pick up a line by boathook. Boat B is to windward of the finger and if she can nudge her way past the end of the finger her bows will then blow in of their own accord. If it is her regular berth there will be dock lines, or a

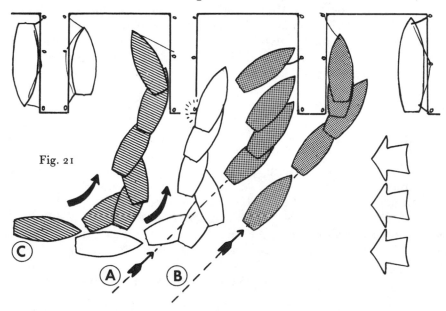

Fig. 21

continuous line, all ready to pick up. Compare this approach to the square-on approach (Fig. 21C) where the over-swing following the right angle turn plus the windage and weathercocking effect leaves the bow pointing downwind. A hard burst ahead on full rudder is necessary to turn her back, but it is risky.

RAFTING ALONGSIDE

Visitors' berths in yacht harbours, marinas and small ports are often crowded and arrivals lie alongside each other, sometimes five or more abreast. There is constant coming and going, boats on the inside or in the middle being extricated and new ones arriving on the outside – easy enough in light weather but tricky in a bit of a breeze.

There are some unwritten rules. All boats should have their own head and stern lines ashore, the biggest craft should be allowed to take the prized inner berth, for the good of all, boats departing from the middle of the heap should always ensure that they secure the gap as they leave, and people crossing the decks of neighbouring craft should always walk via the foredecks to respect their privacy. Much of this is basic sense and manners but there are some snags.

With a wind blowing onshore good fendering is the responsibility of all and every boat should put out her own fenders instead of leaving it to the neighbours. An offshore wind makes everything simpler but a head or stern wind blowing on a rafted group of yachts just emphasises the need for all to have their own lines to the shore. The tendency then is for the whole bunch to slew around, bows or sterns grinding together (whichever is to leeward), and the windward extremities opening and putting a big strain on the headlines. If one boat is moored tighter than the rest she will take all the strain (Fig. 22). Departure from the middle of

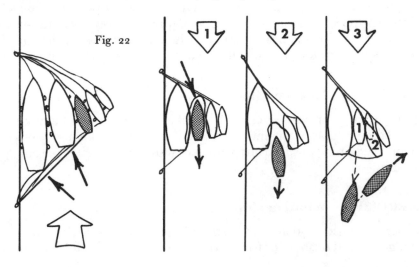

Fig. 22

such a bunch must be done with care, slipping out downwind and closing the bow gap while doing so and before the outer boats begin to take charge. Once the gap opens too wide there is no way to close it again; moreover, if it is daytime many of the other crews may be ashore leaving nobody to handle their boats.

Rafting calls for nimble line-handling and a good deal of anticipation. It is a restless, busy period but also great fun socially and many friends are made while struggling with lines and fenders. It also calls for some tact. There is no way of knowing the expert from the novice until the battle begins; everybody gives orders to everybody else and often it is the loudest voice that carries the day.

EXERCISE 1   Study other people

Spend an hour or so at a busy marina on Sunday evening watching other yachts returning to their berths. Study the following:
Speed of approach.
Readiness of crew.
Number of commands necessary or given.
Amount of engine used to stop her.
Dexterity or otherwise of work with lines.
Success of manoeuvre.
Try to anticipate what the skippers will do next and how the yachts will behave following a tight swing or the use of engine in burst turns or astern.

EXERCISE 2   Springing off

While lying alongside rig a bow spring and experiment to find the right length for it and how the yacht behaves when going ahead against it. Stop, then double back the spring so that it can be slipped from on board. Practise slipping smoothly; see what can happen by over-energetic jerking, also with a rope which has a knot or a clumsy whipping on the end. If it doesn't actually foul up, you will probably see what *might* happen.

EXERCISE 3   Heaving lines

Practise with your regular crew. It can be done as you sail along if you don't fancy people watching. Coil small and throw high. Practise the bowline, making it at speed and with eyes shut. Use a variety of rope types and sizes.

EXERCISE 4   Winding ship

Turn her end-for-end in her berth. If the wind is onshore you won't manage it but if offshore or from either bow or stern it should be possible, unless the berth is too cramped. With the bow line run outside all to the jetty and the stern line laid along it, or vice versa, shove the bow out by boathook and with a fender handy under the stern manipulate the lines to heave her round. This manoeuvre is mainly to give crew experience in handling lines. When you become involved in rafting, line handling plays an important role.

EXERCISE 5   The leeward berth approach
Since it is neither popular, dignified nor wise to exercise in a crowded marina, this one is best done offshore with the anchored mark in clear water. Choose a day when there is a good smart breeze and approach it dead downwind. When the buoy disappears from your view under the bows give her a good hard pull astern. Have someone forward to point where the buoy is. See if her stern throws hard to port. In real circumstances the bows would be allowed to nudge the fendered catwalk or jetty, while the wind continues to blow her tail in.

CHAPTER VI

Anchor Work

Situations

1 A line of moorings occupies the best water in the anchorage. Outside them you'll be in the fairway and it is shallow on the inside. Can you find an anchorage there?

2 The tide is at half ebb as you drop down river. Suddenly the yacht slows to a standstill and the water gurgles merrily around her rudder. She's hard aground. Is there anything you can do?

3 The cable is up-and-down. No matter how you heave and tug it won't give an inch. The anchor is foul. What now?

4 There seemed to be plenty of room when you anchored, but now, with wind against tide, boats are lying at all angles and some are careering around like wild horses. What should you do?

Anchors cannot be taken for granted; their efficiency is not guaranteed under all circumstances and it varies greatly according to the conditions. When we park a car on the handbrake we make allowances, applying it automatically (or not at all) in our garage, with more care on sloping ground, and backing it up by leaving the engine in gear on a hill and perhaps making doubly sure by blocking the rear wheel. Getting back to anchors, the requirements of a sheltered anchorage on a good stiff clay seabed are very different to open water and a dubious holding ground. Then, we may give her double the scope and perhaps use an anchor weight as well as keeping an anchor watch – the brick under the back wheel.

First we must find out how an anchor really works. Of the many types available there is a great variety in terms of efficiency but the almost universal choice is for a burying type anchor. The traditional fisherman anchor with its pickaxe head, used in hard sand, develops around own weight times seven in terms of holding power and thereafter it is liable to begin to drag. If it can lodge a fluke under a rock it will hold indefinitely, but this is not a factor that can be relied upon. The burying types such as the CQR, Danforth, Meon and more lately the Bruce are entirely different in working principle. As load increases and they drag, the design of the palms causes them to plough down through the seabed until completely buried. This presupposes that the seabed is of a nature which allows this to happen. The ideal is hard sand or firm mud; the less than ideal is either oozy mud or gravel in which no anchor holds well, or a hard stony mixture which prevents burying. In stuff of this sort it is the point or points of the anchor which hold and the grip on the seabed is then no better than that of the traditional fisherman type.

In clear waters, usually over a rocky bottom, it is wise to avoid anchoring over dark patches which are probably masses of weed on the seabed, or anchoring too close upwind or up-tide of them. If an anchor is allowed to drag across a weedy patch a cushion of weed can build up under the shank of the anchor which will prevent it from taking a proper hold. On occasions an anchor may seem to be holding well only to let go without warning and thereafter it can skate over the seabed gathering even more weed as it goes. Kelp, bladderwrack and other types of bulky weed are notoriously bad seabed companions for anchors, but in fast tidal waters the finer bright green slub, a hair-like weed, can pose a different problem. Drifting in quite large patches, it collects around an anchor cable and has been known to increase the drag of the current so much that an anchor with a tenuous hold lets go altogether.

In reality, a yacht anchoring in light to moderate winds seldom buries her anchor beyond a few inches of its point(s) and when she swings to wind or current she as likely as not spends a period lying to the bight of her cable, at least if it is chain. If the wind does begin to rise she may well drag for a length before her anchor digs in and buries itself. Likewise in strong tidal currents an anchor may set itself for the ebb in a river and then when the flood begins to run strongly and the yacht swings it may break out and reset itself. More probably it will set in deep to the pull of the stronger current and half-turn in its bed for the opposite pull (Fig. 23).

Scope is the vital factor. Without adequate length of cable to ensure the correct and low angle of drag no anchor can hold its maximum load.

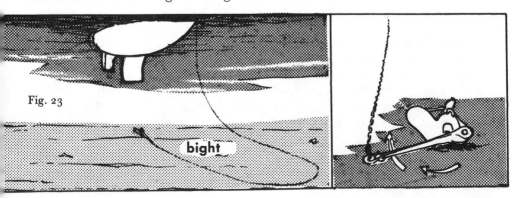

Fig. 23

The oft-quoted minimum is total depth at high water × 3 for chain and total depth × 5 for a rope cable with a 3 fathom chain joiner between anchor and rope. Perhaps 90 per cent of anchoring failures are due to having insufficient scope out. The × 3 and × 5 minimums are indeed *minimums*. In the case of the Bruce one can use less than these scopes provided the boat lies quietly and doesn't sheer around, but one should be prepared to veer as much cable as the boat needs for the conditions and seabed. I have laid to 50 fathoms in 4 fathoms of water with a big fisherman well bedded in hard sand and still dragged it. Had the anchor been a burier it would most probably have held, but there is no guarantee that it would have held with a scope of × 3. It was blowing Force 10 at the time.

The size (weight) of anchor is critical. One cannot lay down a tight table of size per length of boat because windage and hull form bear strongly upon matters of drag. The table in the Appendix is a guide only. What is of greater importance than exactitude is to choose a size nearer to the maximum than the minimum; this is particularly true of small sizes. A lightweight burying anchor may fail to bury if it cannot penetrate a hard crust. The same goes for kedges. Traditionally a kedge is a light anchor, but from time to time it becomes a boy trying to do a man's work. Err on the side of weight. If you can handle it comfortably in and out of the dinghy it is light enough.

CHOICE OF ANCHORAGE

When cruising we tend to look for a sheltered spot, not too far from a landing place and in water which allows us to remain just comfortably afloat and with a clear swing at low tide. We avoid lying in water which is deeper than we need, unless other factors dictate this. We avoid congested areas, open anchorages, poor holding ground, fast tidal areas, deep water, cosy little corners which can become traps if the wind shifts, places close to ferry routes or suchlike, and anchorages which are a very long way from a landing place. Fussy in fact.

Usually we have to settle for any patch of clear water which allows us clear swinging room. Ideally it is completely clear, a circle which has our boat length plus anchor scope as its radius, but more probably we settle for a swinging circle bisected by the swinging circles of other craft. If all swing together all lie clear of each other, but if one boat swings differently there is a chance of collision while at anchor. It is a law of the game that the latest arrival at an anchorage must be the first to shift if swinging circles conflict: she has given the other boats a foul berth (Fig. 24A).

In law, a mooring is a permanent form of anchor and the occupier can only claim prior rights to swing if he is on it. In theory, we can drop anchor close by an unoccupied mooring and if the owner returns, occupies it and hits us in swinging later on *he* is the culprit. I have never heard of anyone enforcing this rule and I hope that I never do (Fig. 24B).

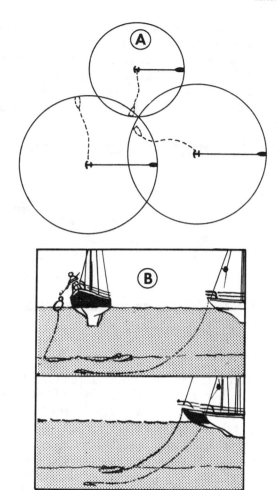

Fig. 24

In an ideal world all boats at anchor would behave the same. In a westerly wind they would lie, say, to the east of their anchors and if there was a current running from left to right they would lie more or less halfway, to the northeast of their anchors. All boats don't behave alike. Shoal draft and high windage powerboats may lie more wind-rode, deep-keeled low windage craft more tide-rode. Long keels, short fins, heavily rigged ketches, sparsely rigged modern sloops – the variety is endless and the outcome unpredictable. A yacht lying to rope swings more freely than another using chain, and with wind against tide some craft begin sheering.

This wind-over-tide situation can only be resolved by each boat having a more than adequate swinging circle, or by anchoring well out of the fast current. It is also a bad time to arrive looking for an anchorage because, at long intervals, generous gaps appear in the otherwise crowded area, tempting places in which to let go. Ten minutes later the newcomer may be set upon from all sides as boats break sheer and come swerving over to close that false gap (Fig. 25). A few generalities can be noted, but they are unreliable. Craft on permanent moorings may have a tighter swinging circle than those at anchor; heavily rigged craft tend to lie more to the wind; long-keeled hulls of traditional design are more prone to wild sheering, usually after lying quietly for awhile; shallow hulls are far more wind-rode than deep ones; a deep hull with a low tophamper may be almost entirely tide-rode.

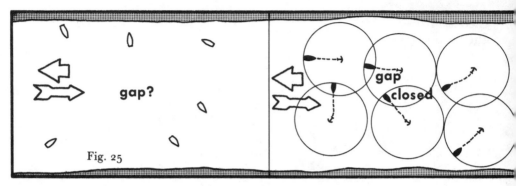

Fig. 25

PLACING THE ANCHOR

It does no harm at all to sail around a bit before making a final choice of a place to let go the anchor. If other craft are lying back to their anchors or on their moorings one can make a shrewd guess at where their anchors are lying on the seabed relative to their bows. In light conditions their chains will hang in a deep bight, shortening the distance between anchor and boat, and in a blow or when wind and tide combine they may be at full stretch. Thus if you should let go close under the stern of the boat ahead and if she later lies back on a longer scope than you'd bargained for, her stern may end up uncomfortably close to your bow. Another advantage of sailing around and sizing things up is that the aspect alters; seen from one angle a usable gap may look better or worse than when seen from another. You can also decide on the direction of your final approach. These days, and faced with a tricky approach, not many people will choose to make it under sail if they have a reliable engine. There's no shame in this; after all, the aim here is to lay an anchor with great precision and the minimum of fuss. Our earlier exercises in handling under power will begin to pay off.

What we are trying to do is position the *yacht*. We can see exactly where we'd like to end up, but where should the anchor be placed to achieve this? This is one of the most difficult of all manoeuvres. The boat must be where we want her, at the end of a proper scope, on an anchor which has bitten in and held.

If the skipper remains at his helm to handle the boat and position her exactly where he wants her to be, he has to make one very important allowance. When *he* feels that the boat is in position for letting go, the anchor is already some 30ft (or whatever the overall length may be) ahead of him. If the boat is still moving ahead when he calls out to let go, the delay while the crew manhandle the anchor overboard and it actually gets to the seabed may account for another half length. Thus the anchor may hit bottom anything from 30 to 40ft ahead of the ideal spot (Fig. 26A).

Or it can be quite otherwise. If the crew take too long and the yacht has lost way, she will have borne off to port or to starboard; and if they then fail to pay out scope quickly enough the anchor will be dragged along the bottom still farther before it bites in and brings them up. This is even more true if anchoring under sail: we have seen how a boat without way on and head-to-wind can pay off and bear away. Knowing these tendencies is halfway to overcoming them.

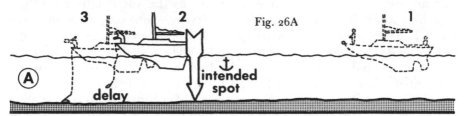

Fig. 26A

Everybody knows the basic rules for anchoring. An approach head to wind, stopping her, letting go and then falling astern while cable is paid out smoothly before snubbing it to strike in the point of the anchor. Nowadays and with burying type anchors there is less need to stop completely. The anchor can be bottomed and then the bows given a small sheer aside to ensure that the cable lies clear of the anchor as the boat falls astern. In wind against tide she can be sheered clear of it, and whatever the conditions it is wise to go astern and bang the anchor in hard, if under engine.

So let's start from the beginning. The cable must run out smoothly, especially chain cable which should be hauled out of the locker for a few fathoms and then allowed to run back, thus clearing it of kinks. Or pull out the scope of chain required and flake it on deck. In smooth waters the anchor can be hung outboard from the stem just clear of the surface, so that it can be got away instantly by throwing off a couple of turns. The skipper draws a mental cross on the water where he wants his anchor to go down.

For most anchorages of around 3–4 fathoms and anchoring say a 30-footer, a rough guide is to try to place the anchor just about two boat lengths ahead of where you want her to bring up finally. In other words, if you expect to put down 12 fathoms of cable (which is 72ft, just over double the boat length) you will be on minimum scope for the depth. It isn't hard to juggle around a bit according to circumstances, making it three lengths or two and a bit as required. The method of sighting ahead along a line from the bow to a point on the mast mentioned earlier in Chapter 2 can help here. A two-length line can be found easily enough – the rest is a matter of judging when you have covered that two lengths ahead (Fig. 26B).

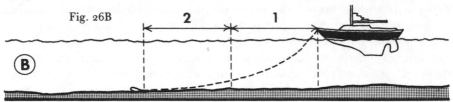

Fig. 26B

A final point on the matter. Successful anchoring is almost fifty per cent in the hands of the crew up forward. He or she must get the anchor down fast and pay out chain or rope smoothly as the yacht falls away, not snubbing at all until she has almost her desired scope out, then snubbing hard. The cable should be seen to rise tautly from the water, and if a hand is placed on it should be felt to shudder and then lie still. The rest of the scope can then be paid out plus a bit for luck at the end. In deep water remember to allow extra time for the anchor to bottom as it has farther to drop and the rarely disturbed chain in the locker runs out less readily than the length in general use. In the unavoidable deep-water anchorage allow double the time for bottoming in say 7 fathoms that you would in 4 or 5.

RECOVERING AN ANCHOR

Stages in anchor recovery are: 1, shortening up; 2, cable up and down; and 3, breaking out. The cable is taken in until the anchor is just safely short of being disturbed and this might mean reducing the scope by half if it is at low tide in an area where tidal range is considerable; the aim is to reduce the time it will take to get the anchor up once the order is given to break out. Stage two, up-and-down, explains itself. One must be careful that the anchor doesn't break out early, as it may in certain types of holding ground. The action of the shank is to act as a lever when raised vertically, twisting the anchor free of its hold. Conversely and in good holding, a burying type may be so deeply buried that it continues to hold even when the cable is up-and-down. The Bruce tends to hang on tenaciously in these conditions.

The actual breakout may be so effortless that the crew don't realise that it has happened, or the yacht may have to be motored over the anchor to break its hold. What is important is that the crew forward should know the state of play all the time. By leaning over the bow and placing a hand or a toe on the taut cable one can feel the breakout at once. He should then give the helmsman a thumbs-up sign to show that it is safe to begin moving ahead. Foredeck work is skilled stuff, especially in any weight of wind or sea. The crew will have to be ready to take a fast turn around the bitts to snub out a recalcitrant anchor, or to veer (let out) cable quickly as ordered.

Breaking out under sail is more complicated. The mainsail may be set and the headsail ready for rapid hoisting. In a breeze it cannot be set until the moment of breaking out is very close because, flogging around, it makes foredeck work practically impossible.

The aim may be to break out on one tack because a moored yacht or whatever prohibits breaking out on the other. Head to wind, a yacht tends to swerve her bows from side to side as the scope is shortened in, alternately pointing to the right tack, the wrong tack and so on. It is the foredeck man's job to see that the headsail goes up in nice time to be held aback and cast the yacht off onto the chosen tack as the anchor breaks. With the headsail backed she will bear off and either break it out, or if it is stubborn, snub on it and cast herself back on the wrong tack (Fig. 27). The foredeck crew knows that she will now almost certainly break out as soon as the chain grows taut: he must be ready to pay out more scope – fast, so that she casts back the wrong way, brings up on her now-holding anchor and swings back yet again in the desired direction. He can now recover the cable as it comes slack and snatch a quick turn to break out the instant it grows up-and-down.

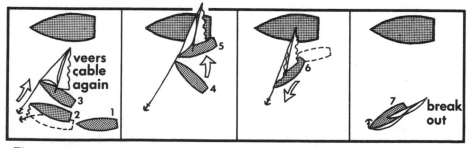

Fig. 27

It is sometimes better to sail the anchor out in the first place. This operation is interesting but it calls for a good, fast foredeck worker. The yacht at the end of her usually full scope is given main and headsail and cast off on the first tack (towards the obstruction if there is one). She will sail out at an angle away from her anchor, trailing slack cable over the seabed until the drag of it begins to slow her at the end of its limit. She is then tacked. She will now be sailing up the length of the cable and the crew hauls in fast – as fast as she is sailing – until the cable begins to come up and down. He must now take a full, fast, secure snubbing turn around cleat or bitts and hang on. The moving yacht should snatch the anchor out of the ground and she is away (Fig. 28).

An anchor over the bow and in the water when under way must be got in quickly (or the yacht slowed) before it can damage her bow and topsides. This is especially important if a sea is running, as it may well be in wind-over-tide conditions.

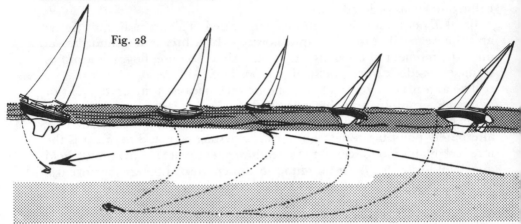

Fig. 28

Breaking out when wind and tide oppose is usually very simple. No sail must be set until the anchor is clear of the ground or all hell will break out as the yacht, in attempting to lie to the wind, begins to sheer on the contrary current. Under bare pole the anchor can be lifted and the yacht can be allowed to stem the current under the windage of mast and hull topsides. She can then be given the headsail, sailed into a clear patch of water and rounded up into the wind for setting the mainsail.

ANCHORING WITH WIND AGAINST TIDE

With wind against tide, anchoring is one of the most troublesome of all situations and there are no ready solutions, as mentioned earlier. It is easy to understand what happens. The hull below water is under the pressure of tidal current while the topsides and rig are under the wind's influence which fluctuates constantly. If the boat was free-drifting she would lie half stern to wind and perhaps make very little way over the

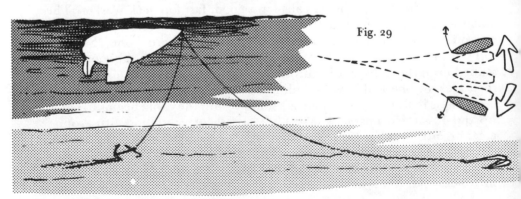

Fig. 29

ground, balanced between the two opposing forces. Because she is tethered by her bow she tries to lie bow to current while the wind drives her to the limit of her scope with pressure from astern. She then begins to slew across the current, 'sailing' off at an angle until her chain brings her up short again. This slewing and sheering process can go on either continually or intermittently. In the latter case she can lie for as long as ten minutes at a time without rampaging off, then she 'breaks sheer' and away she goes.

As we have seen, various craft behave in a variety of ways and if they are moored so closely that their swinging circles intersect, inevitably there will be trouble. It is possible to restrict an individual boat in her gyrations by lowering a second anchor just underfoot, with a little scope (perhaps 2–3 fathoms) so that it acts as a drag (Fig. 29). It is also possible to lay out the second anchor by using the helm to sheer her over to her limit of swing and letting it go (Fig. 30). She is then allowed to lie back and the helm is lashed as shown. Neither of these tricks will stop her from being hit by other craft, though.

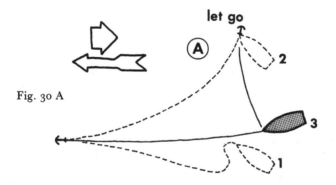

Fig. 30 A

Craft using a rope chain cable are subject to much worse sheering than those on chain only and the use of an anchor weight is often effective in cutting down sheering. The anchor weight was traditionally a pig of ballast borrowed from the bilge, when yachts used to carry trimming ballast. A traveller such as an outsize shackle or a snatchblock was slipped over the anchor cable and the weight was attached to it. By means of a rope tail the weight was then lowered down the cable until it touched bottom. The real reason for doing this is to provide more catenary to the cable and thus maintain a flatter line of pull to the anchor while giving the cable a springiness that reduced shock loads: the result was a greatly increased anchor efficiency. In wind-over-tide conditions an anchor weight provides a seabed drag. As to this weight, there is a marketed article called the Chum, an anchor weight suspended from a large saddle shackle running on the chain. The weight should not be less than say 28 lbs, though, and if heavier is required two such weights should be used rather than trying to struggle a single monster over the bows (Fig. 30B).

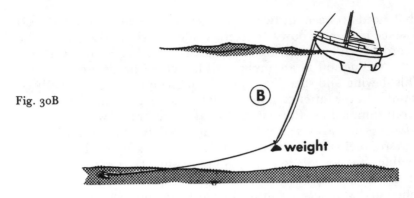

Fig. 30B

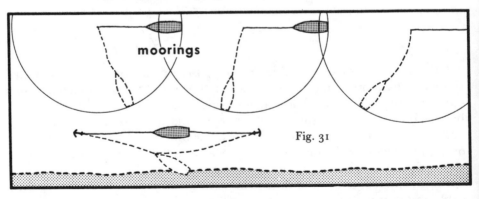

Two of the situations quoted at the beginning of this chapter related to finding a shallow berth inside a line of moorings and to running aground. The third posed the problem of a fouled anchor. All three are common situations in cruising.

MOORING TO A KEDGE

In Fig. 31 we have a sketch of a possible inside berth situation. The moored yachts have swinging circles which bring their outer limits close to the shallows, and in theory there is no room for anyone to anchor between them and the shallows. In steady and continuing onshore winds this is indeed so, but there can as easily be steady and continuing offshore winds, or fickle calms, or the wind dying at sunset.

Fig. 31

The period of ebbing tide is the problem. If a yacht using the inside berth can be held clear of the shallows during the ebb, by laying a kedge, it can be released during the flood because it is of no matter if she does then ground herself. This of course accepts that the bottom is mud or sand, not rocky or otherwise harmful.

Arriving near low water makes things simple because the yacht can be taken into the shallows as close as needs be short of grounding and moored fore-and-aft between bower and kedge, the latter from her stern. Slack water will probably mean the nearby yachts on moorings lying at sixes and sevens with a slight chance of gentle contact unless there is a breeze offshore or along the line to steady them. Throughout the flood all should lie safely clear.

Finding the right spot to anchor is a matter for exploration by echo-sounder. With somebody to call out the depths the skipper can motor to and fro looking for what he has calculated to be the safe minimum depth. Rough transits taken from the shore features will give him a line on his boundaries.

The kedge can either be laid from the dinghy or in a case of this sort more probably it will be laid as part of the anchoring manoeuvre. With the main (bower) anchor set the yacht is motored straight astern for about double the scope required, then the kedge is dropped astern and, going ahead, again, she is middled up between the two. The moor must be as tight as possible.

In a tight berth of this sort, conditions will indicate periods of safe lying with occasional intervals when a watch on deck is required (say, swinging at slack water). Mainly, the skipper must be on the alert for a dominant shift in wind direction.

THE RUNNING MOOR

Mooring between bower and kedge has the disadvantage that when the strain eventually falls on the kedge it will probably drag some distance, being lighter, before it builds up sufficient hold to do its job. Making a running moor with the kedge let go first solves this problem.

First the kedge is hung outside the after pulpit on a slip-line with its cable flaked (*not* coiled) on the cockpit sole or after deck ready to run. On reaching the anchorage the kedge is dropped and the yacht runs straight ahead at a couple of knots, paying out cable until the desired double scope is out, at which point it will have been securely made fast to a strong cleat. The yacht will then be stopped dead in her tracks, first dragging the kedge and striking it deeply into the seabed. Before she can pay off, the main anchor is dropped from the bow and she is middled on both in the normal way. If it is not possible to bang the kedge in by this means, allow extra scope to cater for the wasted scope incurred while dragging it home prior to its biting.

RUNNING AGROUND

It is impossible to cruise for long without accidentally running aground, usually in a river, more rarely on an offshore sandbank, and more rarely still on a rocky outcrop. This last danger is dealt with in Chapter 12 on emergencies; it is the harmless but tiresome grounding in sheltered water that we will deal with first.

Grounding on the flood tide presents few problems unless it is on a lee shore in a fresh breeze, when the problems will be to keep from driving farther on. Usually one simply lowers the sails and hauls her off under power, stern first. If the shore is flat and there is no haste, the anchor can be let go with just enough scope out to allow her to swing on it as the tide makes.

To ground on a flat lee shore on a falling tide is a very different matter – and at half ebb when the level is falling at its fastest rate, different yet again. Only by working at dizzy speed and by good luck will she come off. If she does not respond to the engine full astern (sails down) within the first half minute it is usually useless; you put the kettle on and prepare for a long wait.

With a moderate 12 ft range of tide, at mid-ebb, the level of the water will be falling at a rate of about an inch in 68 seconds. A long-keeled hull will stick fast within five minutes of going on. A fin-keeler, if she can be heeled and dragged off quickly stands a chance – a twin-keeler no chance at all. The practice of running out a kedge to deeper water as a last-ditch effort rarely works, unless it is undertaken at once; and it will have to be quick.

With a kedge laid well off the bows can sometimes be hauled right round and a fin keel hull then often responds, with crew hanging out to heel her the while. 'Sugging' or running from side to side to work up a regular rolling motion helps in soft mud since it breaks keel suction (Fig. 32A).

To run off the kedge is a job for the best dinghy hand aboard. If he will have to row off across the current dragging a long warp from the grounded yacht, he will be taxed to the limit. Time spent in rapidly flaking it down into the dinghy pays off because he will then pay it out astern instead of dragging it. There will be no time to do tricky things by way of suspending the kedge from the dinghy stern – the correct procedure. He will have to pile aboard, take the kedge, flake the warp, grab the oars and row like hell. It is very important to run out far more scope than depth requires because distance will be lost in the interval between shipping the oars and dropping the kedge overboard, and still more distance as it drags home prior to biting. Haste is vital but let's not forget safety. A heavy kedge round one ankle and a tumble overboard is all it takes.

DRAGGING

From time to time every anchor drags. It is a measure of the vigilance of her crew that they become aware of it (or aware of the likelihood) in good time to avoid any unpleasant consequences. We must have some idea of the nature of the seabed before we go sticking anchors into it. The chart tells us in general terms what to expect, if the abbreviations are noted and understood. Some almanacs and, for example, Admiralty chart 5011 (a booklet, really) give this information in full.

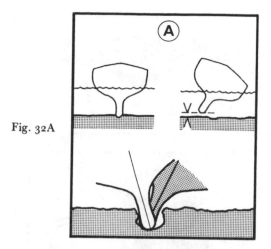

Fig. 32A

Scope we have dealt with. If the holding is less than ideal we veer more cable, and we tug the anchor home under engine; if it holds, breaks out, holds again and so on then we know that the anchorage is not to be trusted in anything more than a light breeze.

With chain and to a lesser extent with rope plus chain there will be a good deal of rumbling and grumbling loudly audible below whenever a boat swings to the turn of tide. The long bight of cable is being dragged over the uneven seabed and boat acoustics greatly magnify the sounds. The only sure way to set doubts at rest is to feel the cable. Rest a hand on it: if it is dragging it will grow taut, rise from the water, sag suddenly with vibration, tauten again and so on.

Now and again, fortunately rarely, we have to lie in a poor anchorage overnight and an anchor watch is necessary. Watchkeepers must know what they are supposed to be watching. Bearings taken on shore lights or buoy lights at right angles to the potential line of drag are the first guide. House or similar lights are useless because people tend to go to bed and put their lights out. This may mean that no lights of any sort are available and the 'watch-lead' must be used. An ordinary hand lead or any similar heavy weight is lowered to the seabed on a light line which is left slack enough to allow for the side-to-side and fore-and-aft driftings of a yacht at anchor. If she really begins to drag, the line will of course grow taut and give warning. By attaching the inboard end to a cleat and taking a bight of line around, say, a frying pan, the tightening of the line will drag it down with a warning clatter (Fig. 32B). Allowance must be made at long intervals for rising tide or the swing of tide at high or low water. Incidentally, this frying pan warning can be used as a depth indicator, if the weight is adjusted to hang below the boat, held by a turn on a cleat but with the frying pan suspended over the companionway, the slackening of the line when the weight begins to rest on the seabed will cause the pan to bang down with enough noise to arouse the dozing watch.

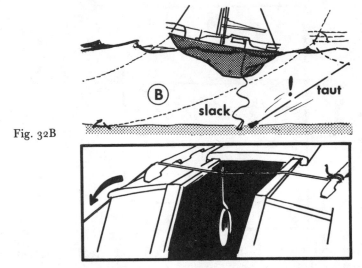

Fig. 32B

Any likelihood of dragging caused by a strengthening and shifting wind during the night, changing a sheltered anchorage into an open one, means getting out at once. If the way out is via a narrow gap between banks or rocks this can be dangerous: it is vital to chart a safe course before turning in; moreover it should be general enough to permit safe departure from anywhere within the swinging circle.

FOULED ANCHORS

One of the regular consequences of dragging is fouling the anchor by picking up some seabed obstruction. Old chains, wires and general junk abound in many creeks, particularly those which sheltered wartime craft long ago. It pays to have a good hard pull and to motor against the imprisoned anchor before resorting to science because the obstruction may well be a short length of something or other which is silted up. Once freed it can be raised to the surface and cleared. Usually one can pass a light line under the obstruction by first tying the end to a bottle or similar float, then poking it down on the boathook so that the bottle can float up on the other side, taking the end of the line up with it. Taking the weight of the obstruction, 'hanging off' as it is called, allows the anchor to be eased away and fall clear.

If the anchor is truly foul, first try motoring the cable around in a tight circle: it just may come clear. Don't waste time if it doesn't clear right away. Haul the cable taut up and down and prepare a chain collar (**Fig. 33**). The trick now is to feel the collar down over the shank of the anchor (and it is surprising how easy it is to do this by touch) and then simultaneously slack away the anchor cable while pulling up on the collar line. If this doesn't work, get the dinghy afloat and try tugging ahead on the collar line, again simultaneously with slackening off the cable.

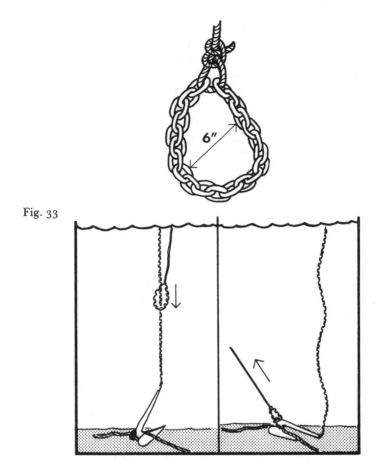

Fig. 33

Much depends on the depth. Things can be done in a couple of fathoms that are impossible in four or five. Working at low water, it may be possible to hang off the obstruction as described. Also, a second anchor prepared with a tripping line can be used, deliberately fouling the same obstruction to allow the first anchor to be dipped free, then clearing the second on its tripping line. We have been considering plough and similar anchors so far; a fouled fisherman can often be cleared by sweeping the seabed with a length of chain between two dinghies or yacht and tender, after slipping and buoying the fouled cable.

TRIPPING LINES

There is a fair amount of argument about the use of anchor tripping lines and buoys. While their use is a good insurance against the risk of fouling, the modern fin-and-skeg rudder or twin-keel and spade rudder designs offer an excellent chance of the yacht fouling her own tripping line and then tripping out her own anchor at turn of tide. Alternatives to the surface floating buoy (usually a plastic fender) are to make the line so short that the buoy is permanently under water and below the keel. There will then only be the lesser problem of hitching on to the buoy at low water, with a boathook, and then dropping a running noose down the boathook and over the buoy.

Another method is to secure the end of the tripping line, slackly, to the cable far enough up to be reachable when up-and-down. A third is to dispense with the buoy and use a length of floating rope. There is a risk that such an unbuoyed rope may be a trap for the propellers of innocent passing strangers. Use tripping lines when it seems wise and with full awareness of the penalties, especially at turn of tide.

REDUCTION TO SOUNDINGS

The calculation of depth at various states of tide is a pitfall for many cruising yachtsmen and the delight of mathematicians. The following notes are not aimed at the latter, who will make a fine meal of it and achieve great accuracy no matter what I say.

What we need to know is how much depth will be left to us at low tide and therefore whether we will lie afloat. We also may need to know what the total depth will be at high water in order to veer sufficient scope of cable before turning in. No matter how precise our calculations there is no guarantee that the actual depth will be as predicted – wind-driven tide, barometric pressure and the topographical nature of the anchorage all affect the rise and fall. For instance a sharp barometric rise of one inch can mean a fall in predicted tidal height of up to one foot and vice versa; the range of a tide (vertical distance between consecutive high and low water levels) can be significantly less at the top end of a creek which has a narrow outlet to the sea, and the navigator may not have published information at hand to warn him.

Thus we aim always to err on the safe side. We will assume that the reader knows the mechanics of tidal movement, the difference between Range and Height, Mean Level and Chart Datum and so on. Suppose, then, that we are entering a strange river or anchorage of some sort and we need to know what the *least* depth of water can be for us to anchor and expect to stay afloat at all times. If we go in at dead low water there is no problem, except to know what the total depth will be at high tide and how much scope to veer.

The appropriate tide table for that day it will tell us the *height* to expect. If we add this figure to the depth in which we are lying we will get an inaccurate answer but one which errs on veering a bit more cable than we need if the tides are at neaps and near enough the right amount if they are at springs.

An arrival at half ebb or half flood means that at low water there will be less depth by half the range. The proper way to tackle this problem is to find the range for the day, halve it and add depth above and below chart datum. If things are happening rather quickly there won't be much time to start consulting tables and doing sums. The simplest and safest method is to take a quick glance at the tide tables, note the highest figures shown, which will be the top springs and therefore near enough the total range ever found in those parts, and simply halve it. That will be the amount of depth you're going to lose, so you'll want a bit more than that in order to stay afloat.

It might go like this: your finger runs down the tables and 5 m seems to be the highest tide shown. It is half ebb so we'll bargain to lose $2\frac{1}{2}$ m. The yacht draws 5 ft (call it 2 m for luck) and so we want to find a depth of $4\frac{1}{2}$ m. Being human and only half metricated we'd probably call this a flat 3 fathoms. If it was a neap period we would know that we would end up with more water below us at low tide and who is going to argue?

For very rough calculations like these we assume that the period of an ebb or a flood is 6 hours (it is more than that) and that the level will rise or fall one-quarter of the range by the first 2 hours, half the range by the third, and three-quarters by the fourth hour. (Fig. 34A illustrates this.)

Fig. 34A

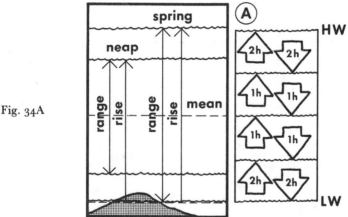

We can also arrive at range by using the Mean Level (ML) figure shown for that area in the almanac in the Tidal Differences sections. Mean Level is just what it sounds like – the half-tide level which remains constant no matter how far above or below it the tide 'ranges'. To find the range from ML on a particular tide, we simply double the ML figure and subtract the height for the day: the result is the height of *Low Water* above Chart Datum. Subtract this from height and we get range. If we only need to know range, then it is easier still. Height minus Mean Level times 2. For example: Height 4 m and ML 2.2 m, so $4 - 2.2 = 1.8 \times 2 = 3.6$ m range.

Now and again, at some stage of the final approach to the anchorage it is possible to fix the yacht's position exactly. Perhaps a transit of shore marks while bringing a prominent land feature abeam gives an exact position on the chart. Provided the nature of the seabed is fairly constant – not subject to shifting with winter gales and thus variations in depth – we can relate the depth shown on the chart at that spot to the *actual* depth as shown by the echosounder. This means that as we will be seeking an anchorage within a very short time afterwards, the difference between charted and actual depth can be used in finding an anchorage. Chart may show 6 m, echosounder shows 9 m or in other words we have 3 m more than the chart shows at that time. If it happens to be within an hour or so either side of low water the level isn't going to change very much and we can safely prospect around for a charted 2 m or less. By finding the range for the day we can be a little more accurate.

The rule of thumb is to multiply that day's rise by 2 and subtract the mean spring rise. Suppose the tide table shows a figure of 4.5 m, spring rise 5 m, then $4.5 \times 2 - 5 = 4$ m range.

The rise being 4.5, we can subtract range and come up with a modest 0.5 m above chart datum at low tide. Chart figures show depth *below* chart datum. Suppose the chart soundings shown are 3 m: the depth at low water would then be 3.5 m on that particular tide (Fig. 34B). See the Appendix for reduction of soundings.

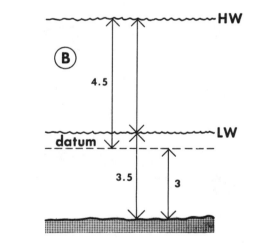

Fig. 34B

EXERCISE 1   Feeling the cable

Drop the anchor in about 3 fathoms and with the engine slow astern pay out a little cable. Take a turn. Note the behaviour of the cable as it drags. Pay out small amounts of cable, feeling at intervals. Note the moment when the anchor begins to bite, holding and dragging by turns. Pay out full required scope and go hard astern on it. Note how the cable rises and tautens.

EXERCISE 2 Judging scope ahead

Bend a line with a buoy onto the anchor, just long enough for the buoy to reach the surface. Anchor normally to the correct scope. Stand at the helm and, looking forward, note the position of the buoy against the mast. With the engine slow astern, stretch the cable taut and note the new position of the buoy against the mast. Tape the mast for future reference.

EXERCISE 3 Judging position

Lay your anchored mark in clear water. Noting wind direction and current, try to place the anchor in the position which when full scope is out will bring your stern close to the float. This is extremely difficult. Try it under engine and if you feel adventurous try it under sail. Take your due share of the hard work in recovering the anchor at each attempt. The most difficult conditions will be when the wind is at right angles to or against the current. In the latter instance it is almost impossible to judge the final position the yacht will take up.

EXERCISE 4 Signals

Evolve with your regular crew some simple hand signals for communication between cockpit and foredeck when working anchors. Examples: hand straight up when cable is up-and-down; backward-waving motion tells helmsman to slow or cut engine; downwards wave of fingers for slow down; finger and arm straight and pointing in direction of cable lead; thumb up for anchor broken out. Waving left or right indicates how bows should be turned.

EXERCISE 5 Sailing out an anchor

This exercise has great fun value. Only the best hand should be handling the anchor and cable because it can be risky. Don't try it in more than a moderate breeze.

EXERCISE 6 Anchoring under sail

The yacht can be brought up under mainsail only. The drill to perfect is the smooth running of the cable and smart lowering of the mainsail as the yacht loses headway and begins to fall off. Snub the cable when about half the full required scope is out, let it run again, and snub for a full due when the full scope is out.

EXERCISE 7   Raising anchor under sail

Decide which tack you wish to clear on. Shorten up. Make ready to hoist
and back the headsail. Haul in and hoist. Be ready to reverse the helm if
she breaks out and drops astern.

EXERCISE 8   Running off a kedge

Sometime when lying quietly to anchor see how quickly you can run off a
kedge. Dinghy alongside, flake down warp in it after lowering in the
kedge, row out to limit of kedge warp (end secured on yacht), let go kedge.
Note what went wrong, and how soon the kedge bites on hauling it in.
Note how much scope is left: remember that if you want to haul off on a
kedge, the scope will decrease as the yacht is drawn towards it, so a very
generous initial scope is needed.

EXERCISE 9   Exploring the depth

Prior to anchoring in a creek or close inshore, run in a slow, flat zig-zag,
inshore, offshore, inshore etc. Note the pattern of depth changes, and
distant marks in line when over the best water. This technique is important
when anchoring close to shallows. The bottom may rise steeply within
your swinging circle – a snare should the wind shift on the ebb.

EXERCISE 10   Estimating the depth

Using the method for determining range for the day, choose a spot on the
chart in soundings and while on the way to it try to estimate what *actual*
depth there will be as compared to charted soundings.

CHAPTER VII

Pilotage

Situations

1 Convection fog lies along the river, visibility down to 100 yards. The ebb has begun and it is time to leave; there is every chance that the fog will clear by mid-morning. The channel is well buoyed. How will you proceed?

2 Approaching the coast at a sharp angle after a night passage. The expected headland looms ahead through the morning haze but it is less prominent than you expected. 'Shoaling, shoaling!' calls a voice from below as somebody switches on the echosounder. What has gone wrong?

3 The chart shows three buoys in a triangle, but when he raises them on the horizon ahead they are strung out in a long line and widely separated. Where on earth can he be?

Pilotage is 90 per cent 'looking' until fog closes down, and then it is 50 per cent listening and 50 per cent attention to set and drift. In pilotage one sails from point to point. We can adjust logs and compasses to the point of near-accuracy and known error, and steering carefully we can hold the heading we have plotted and run our distances to within a tenth of a nautical mile. What we cannot do with any exactitude is to establish the exact rate and set of the tide, the surface drift or our own leeway. If we plot and steer with all our care and, having made an allowance for set and drift, if we then take nothing for granted and allow a generous margin for error, nothing very terrible should happen.

We move from point to point or from fix to fix. By 'points' I mean established and unquestionable positions such as headlands, lightships and beacons which provide exact point of departure or arrival. Fixes are as good as circumstances permit. There is a growing tendency to rely almost entirely upon RDF fixes in modern cruisers, accepting poor fixes as readily as good ones. The advice of Lt Cdr Bill Anderson, Cruising Secretary of the Royal Yachting Association, sums up the question of fixes. 'Better', he says, 'to plot a position which is the result of several methods than to use only one and trust entirely to its accuracy.' An RDF bearing, crossed by a log distance, confirmed by echosounder and supported by a rather woolly extreme range compass bearing is probably a far safer bet than one clear RDF fix which may have a hidden error due to atmospheric interference or a wrongly read compass card. Just because three lines intersect together is no reason to suppose that the fix is a good one.

Eyeball navigation – looking – is simple and relaxing until something doesn't quite add up; until a headland refuses to lie in transit with the next headland or a buoy appears where none should be. Then all hell breaks loose. A combination of looking and plotting is the only safe answer. One must always have a course to steer so that, at a pinch, we know where we have *been*. The practice of working backwards along the plot in order to see where we have got to has been the saving of many a navigator.

PILOTING BY EYE

Provided we know where we are on the chart and how we are heading, we cannot be lost. In coastal pilotage the navigator is presented with a constantly changing prospect of headlands, bays, straight strands, towns, buoys, beacons, islands and so on. As he passes by them their angles to him and to each other change continually and depending on his distance off and the distances between one feature and the next these angles alter quickly or slowly. The navigator must translate the three-dimensional coastline to the one-dimensional chart and back again as he stares from one to the other. Stop reading and take a look around the room. The left hand edge of a chair back may be in transit with a cupboard handle a few inches behind it and with the base of a picture on the wall ten feet behind it. Move your head a few inches: the close-to transit alters widely and the

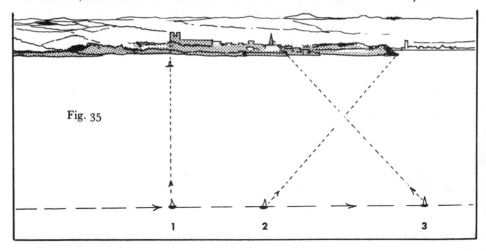

Fig. 35

distant one hardly at all. If you get to your feet and take two paces in any direction both transits vanish and that chair back is realigned with new and different objects. The one certain feature is the chair back.

In coasting, a single identified feature between you and the shore has a similar role to play. When it lines up with a second identifiable feature you have a reliable position line which in crossing your courseline gives a reliable fix. As your boat moves forward and the offshore feature moves back, it can be used to identify shore marks and provide a series of position lines, until such time as it is too far astern to be of further use. By then you have chosen a new pointer (Fig. 35).

Objects don't always need to fall into line. Once identified beyond doubt their relative position seen halfway across a bay or river mouth, or an equal distance to seaward of a point to that of a prominent (charted) building inshore of it, gives another rough position line (Fig. 36A). In passing let me mention the illusory effect of some headlands. If the chart shows a sheer fall into the sea a bearing or a line can be taken of it, but if a low water reef or stretch of beach is shown it is often hard to know where the headland actually ends (Fig. 36B).

Fig. 36

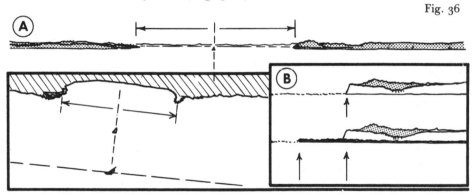

A coastline is full of tricks. Situations 2 and 3 are typical examples. In one case a false headland and in the other a mistake made in relating scale of chart to actual distances. Every headland has three different aspects, frontal and viewed from left or right. From one direction it may stand our boldly, from another it is lost against its background, and from the third it may have a dominant feature such as a distinctive row of cottages or a pine woods which is peculiar to that headland alone. Depending upon the angle of approach from seaward or along the shore it can show any of these faces. We may have a memory of it as a bold precipitous bluff and when an unspectacular coastal bulge appears it is easy to be mislead.

Following the coast is rather like listening to music while following the score. Making a landfall is like coming into a concert in the middle of a piece: unless one knows the music it can be difficult to find the right place in the score. This is why a landfall made in the centre of a featureless stretch of coast so often raises problems. A typical case might be an inshore tack when beating coastwise. The coast is approached at an angle and the navigator becomes obsessed with the need to identify it. If he is to continue inshore there is good reason to do so but if he is about to make another 30 mile tack offshore into open water it doesn't matter a damn. On the other hand it is better to lay a course for a prominent and recognizable feature even if it adds a few miles to the distance. At night it is easier. A lighthouse with a 20 mile range gives the navigator a 40 mile target.

Visibility is a key factor in coastal recognition. In clear visibility a peak which is 40 miles inland may be the first thing he sees, as it appears over the horizon. If he was expecting to see a level stretch of cliffs he may be baffled. Conversely, in less ideal conditions the peak will not be seen and the foreground level stretch of cliffs merges with an undulating middle ground: a wise navigator makes no pronouncements. He keeps his mouth closed and his options open.

The coastline shifts and alters, stands sharply clear in a mass of detail or fades to a series of greys and greens according to the time of day and the effect of shadows, or the brilliance of colours brought out by recent rain and sudden sunshine. The only rules are never to expect a coastal feature to look exactly as it did the last time you saw it, never to guess at the identity of a church spire or similar 'conspic' feature, and remember that a new caravan camp on a hillside 30 miles away can be mistaken for the white buildings of a lighthouse.

If coastal features are misleading, offshore buoyage can be more so. The angle of approach is the key to the whole thing. In Situation 3 our navigator has not realised that although the three buoys shown on his chart appear to be grouped in a cosy little triangle, they are in fact a mile or so apart. He does not see them in a triangle because he is seeing them from almost sea level. Place three small objects, peas maybe, in a well-spaced triangle on the table and view them from table level: you see two of them closer and the third at more distance, but you see them as a line.

When we sail we are at the centre of a circle of horizon which depending on height of eye may be 3–4 miles away. Thus we see objects either inside or on the circle, or beyond it as we go along; nonetheless they will be ranged around us in a circle. With navigation buoys and according to their size and height we see them first at extreme range just outside our horizon, perhaps half dipped below it and shapeless with distance. Then they assume shape and later colour. In conditions of sunlight and back-lighting they remain black and when the sun is behind the viewer the colours and details may be visible at almost extreme range. As we coast, then, buoys appear ahead and on either hand as a series of peppercorns. A large buoy at a distance may appear similar in size to a closer but smaller one; buoys with the coastline behind them may not be seen at all until they are much closer still. The horizon buoys all appear to be strung out around our horizon circle like beads on a string, yet all lie at different angles to us and each other.

Having identified one of them and knowing our position on the chart, we have a line of position which should unravel the puzzle. A plotted bearing allows us to reverse the procedure. With a position on the chart we can see what other buoys should bear from where we are, and then armed with the bearings of two or three other buoys we can sweep the horizon with a hand bearing compass, locating them as we go.

The temptation is to buoy-hop and let the chartwork go hang. You *must* have a heading for the steering compass all the time. While steering for the next mark in the series it is possible to be side-set by the tide and end up steering for an entirely different and *wrong* buoy.

Beware of seeing what you *want* to see. The mark which comes up when it should and where it should is not necessarily the one it should be. At night it is easier, but at extreme range and glimpsed between rain showers a distant light dipping in the swell can give a false light sequence; you may be expecting to see a Group 5 and see it you do, just once. Not until later do you discover to your alarm that it must have been a continuous 1 second flash. With experience, a buoy at extreme distance, barely or not seen at all by beginners, may be identified (subject to confirmation) by some split-second gleam or a momentary impression of shape as it tosses and heaves. It is not so much seeing as the subconscious knowledge of what to *expect* to see when it comes to spotting a buoy at the limit of visual range.

It is one of the more sour twists of fate that our navigation is at its most accurate best when we probably need it least and at its worst when we need it most. Coasting or on passage in calm sunlight our charts are models of precise plotting, but hammering to windward at night, in slashing rain and a rising sea, it becomes a soggy and inaccurate gamble. It should *not* be so but so often it is so. This is a very good reason to strive for accuracy whenever we can: our standards then have less distance to fall.

The next best thing to knowing exactly where we are is knowing just how far adrift we *might* be. The cone of probability. As we sail farther from our starting point a deviation from the plotted line becomes greater. If we are 1° off course, at the end of 60 miles we will be 1 mile out. This would be quite good going though, and the error is more likely to be a compound of a bit of this and a bit of that. Compass error, a steering tendency, underestimation of leeway or a tidal set in excess of the predicted rate could well add up to 4° or more – 2 miles adrift in 30, an important mark missed and another (wrong) one appearing dead ahead just to fool us (Fig. 37).

What gets us off the hook again and again without our knowing it is that these errors are rarely all in the same direction; the helmsman may be luffing above his course but that stronger tidal set might counter it. Some errors we can fix and others we have to hunch. First get the compass right.

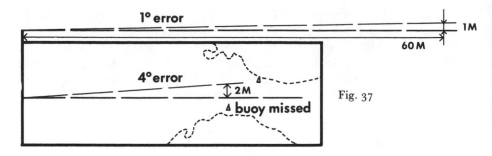

Fig. 37

Without going mad about terrestial magnetism, causes of deviation, pivot friction and the rest, what can be done by way of a compass check? Swinging is covered in the Appendix but headings can be checked quite easily at any time; then if a proper swing is called for it can be carried out. The ideal would be a known position in the middle of a river mouth or a small bay, such as a reliable buoy or a beacon with deep water all round it.

With a large scale chart of the area first note a series of shore marks – churches, ends of wharves, points of land, in fact any features which can be seen on both the land and the chart and which are precise positions ashore. Slack water is needed. Knowing the magnetic headings from the mid-bay buoy to each of the shore marks, we then motor slowly towards each in turn, keeping the buoy between us and the mark as a transit. If for instance buoy to church on the chart (having brought the given variation up to date if necessary) if 043° Magnetic and our steering compass reads 046°, we can conclude that we have 3° westerly deviation on that heading.

It is unlikely that any bay or river entrance will sport us a complete set of bearings right round the compass, but we can reuse the same bearings as

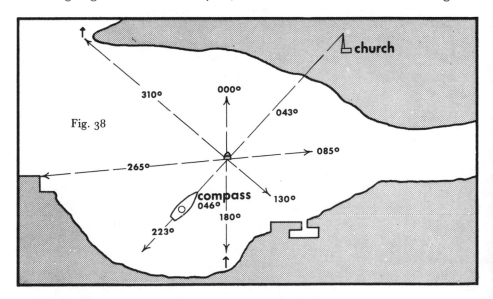

Fig. 38

back bearings. This isn't easy because it means looking over your shoulder to keep the marks in line, but two people can do it if conditions are calm and tideless (Fig. 38). Our 043° becomes 223° on the chart and the compass may show a corresponding deviation. In addition to this form of check, useful transits will come up constantly while sailing and it is quite simple to build up a complete set of headings. Be careful to avoid using buoys if there is some chance of their having dragged from their positions and remember that buoys at close range in any case have a fairly wide arc of 'wander' around their charted positions.

The boat's log may be a towed Walker or a through-hull electronic type, but the trailing rotator of a good Walker seems to hold its own for accuracy and most long-distance yachtsmen seem to carry a Walker as a spare whatever else they may have. The boundary layer of water along a hull gives rise to certain effects which can lead to inaccurate readings, which the rotator towed well astern does not, although the latter is subject to wave forces in rough weather which may call for allowances to be made.

A log can be calibrated by making timed runs over a measured mile (see Appendix) and it is wise to do this at the start of the season in any case. Log checks can also be made during the ordinary course of cruising. Whenever a straight run between known points can be made at slack water or tide change, the distance on the chart should be noted against that by log. If a notepad is kept for the purpose a pattern will begin to emerge. Each entry should also give wind and sea conditions, and in the case of a single through-hull transducer, whether the yacht was hard on the wind on a particular tack. This rather random system of checking log accuracy has the advantage of revealing any side effects due to sailing conditions, which a flat-water run over a measured mile will not show.

Echosounders with a single transducer to one side of the keel are also subject to malfunction when heeling, the spread of the signal being open and clear on one tack and partly blocked by the keel on the other. Two transducers and a changeover is far superior; the alternative is to luff occasionally to bring the boat upright for a correct reading.

Helm errors are human errors. Instruments make no bones about telling lies, but people do. The worst thing a navigator can do is to show exasperation for a badly steered course. The sensible thing to do is to go below after a helmsman has been on duty for ten minutes or so and sit quietly holding the hand bearing compass in your lap. It doesn't matter that this compass may be reading incorrectly due to below-deck deviation; you can see at once whether the helmsman is hunting to one side of his given course, and if it is consistent and not excessive allow for it. Bawling at the helmsman will only invite hot denials and friction all round. A gentle 'What's your course now?' is hint enough.

Tidal set and rate errors are impossible to predict. Strong winds which have prevailed for some days can produce surface drift and this can accelerate or reduce the rate of tide to a marked degree. On any cross-tide course which involves leaving a buoy dead astern, a series of careful back bearings can sometimes indicate the rate of set, or whether an allowance made for tide is about right. It is always interesting at the end of a passage to see where you have fetched up. The course may have been laid to one side of a distant light vessel, perhaps: in the course of time it appears on the horizon dead ahead and the navigator swells out his chest. In fact, and remembering that the light vessel is still some 8 or so miles ahead, had he held on to his plotted course he might have come up to it on the wrong side – an error of perhaps half a mile or more. In fog that half mile could have raised problems. Remember the set of the tide and whether it would ultimately have put the yacht where she should have been, or whether it would have done quite the opposite. Always try to account for errors. Instruments, helmsman, tidal or bad plotting, there is always a reason.

KNEECAP NAVIGATION

It is a feature of small boat navigation and pilotage that a good deal of it is carried out under difficulty. A proper chart table is more important than a proper galley, and even a good chart table becomes impossible to use at times. At navigation classes ashore we sit at firm, level tables and at sea we are cramped and at the mercy of motion. Worse than the physical difficulty of hanging on to flying pencils is the numbing effect on the brain induced by noise, motion and perhaps queasiness. The easier and simpler the chart problems can be made the safer all round.

In steady conditions chartwork can be as refined as you please. In rough conditions it is safer to settle for less accuracy and to make due allowance for this. It would be hazardous to try for pin-point accuracy in making a landfall in shoal-infested waters; better to detour a little in order to fetch up at some clearly seen landmark.

One of the biggest errors we can make at the chart table is to apply variation the wrong way round when converting from or to True north. Unless we have learned from the beginning to work in True on the chart and convert back and forth almost subconsciously when using the magnetic compass, unless it has become instinctive to do so, it is an added burden and an invitation to error to try it in bad weather when the brain is under strain. Heresy though it might be, it is safer to work exclusively from the chart magnetic rose.

Thus a navigator needing a new course from the mark he has just brought abeam can slap his rules on the chart and read from the magnetic rose, getting a course to steer which at most may be a degree out (if his chart is reasonably up to date). He can apply any necessary deviation from a foolproof card, e.g. 'for North *steer* 003°' etc, and he can then consider whether an allowance for tidal set is needed by taking his current atlas up on deck with him.

Having decided whether the set is from ahead, astern or on the bow, beam or quarter he can hunch on the rate and consult the table of approximations in the Appendix. The errors likely from such casual navigation won't be large and for courses of up to 10 miles they are acceptable under the circumstances. The *possibility* of a gross error by trying to achieve high accuracy is potentially more dangerous. An error of perhaps 3° in 10 miles amounts to about half a mile. If the visibility is average to good the mark ahead should appear soon enough for a correction to be made. What is of the greatest importance is that if errors are known to exist, the target should be correspondingly safe and easy to spot. If it isn't, then it is folly to proceed in that direction (Fig. 39).

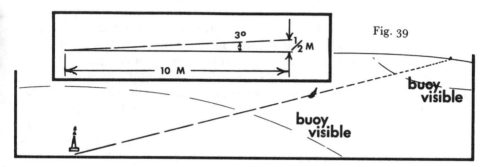

Fig. 39

Kneecap navigation is often forced upon us. When the navigator aboard is also the skipper and the most skilled helmsman there are times when he must be in two places at once. For instance, we had left Ostende bound across the North Sea for home when the wind forecast as Force 4 jumped to Force 7 on the nose. We had threaded some 20 miles of offshore sandbanks but I decided to turn back and head for Zeebrugge. The course was a torturous one among the banks, buoy-to-buoy but with a wild following sea due to shoal water. My crew couldn't handle the boat, or navigate with the accuracy required in the frantically gyrating conditions below. I had to manage with the folded chart by my side, one-handed using the parallel rules and allowing for a substantial cross-tide partly by eye and partly by estimation. The whole thing was fairly typical. (Other such occasions might be the approach to a port among busy shipping, or navigating in waters where seeing is as important as plotting.)

Courses between buoys averaged about 2–3 miles which meant that I was never long out of sight of the buoy astern before the next ahead was in view. The buoy astern was the one I *knew* and it was more important than the one ahead, yet to be identified with certainty. When the speed of the boat is double the speed (rate) of the tide on the beam, one must steer up-tide 30° to counteract it; when the boat speed is four times the tide rate on the beam one steers up 15°. We were making 6 knots and I guessed the tide rate as 2 knots, so I steered up some 20°. I also kept glancing astern to see how the buoy astern lay in relation to my port quarter rail. Very rough, but it served to maintain a good enough heading over short distances.

With the tidal set 45° on bow or stern the lay-off is 20° when boat speed is double tidal rate. Rough, very rough, but used intelligently and with one's options wide open it serves in a tight spot.

SPEED

There is a good argument in favour of making a passage plan based on an average speed made good. Provided one doesn't set this speed too high and condemn the ship's company to hour upon hour of motoring it has a lot in its favour. The speed under sail alone, in typical summer weather, of a 25 ft cruiser might be as little as 3 knots when averaged over some days of cruising. On an individual passage it could be anything from 5 down to 1 knot. Therefore a realistic average to aim for with a boat of this size could be 4 knots in fast sailing weather and 3 knots in calmer conditions.

What this means in main effect is that the navigator can plan when he prefers to cross a busy shipping lane, when he would like to make his landfall, and when to arrive at a prominent headland in order to catch the fair tide. The pitfall lies in the temptation to press on faster and faster. An early arrival at the headland sows the idea of catching the next tide fair at the next headland by motoring just a little bit faster, and this destroys the whole idea and pleasure of cruising under sail.

The enemy of accuracy under sail is the combination of light, fickle headwinds and fast spring tides. The many small course alterations become impossible to plot accurately and the hourly alteration in current rate and direction, plotted on the rather small scale of a passage chart, is too clumsy for accuracy. The simple answer is to motor straight and steady, applying tidal set at intervals of three hours or so, making no attempt to allow for them but noting the distance to which the yacht has been set either side of her rhumb line. When the end of the passage is within reach a course alteration to allow for remaining hours of set can then be made (Fig. 40).

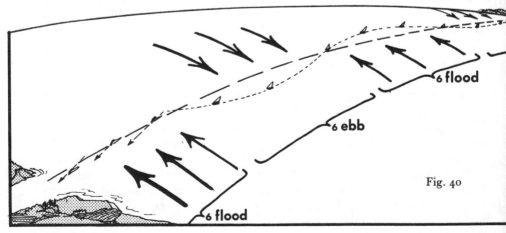

6 flood

6 ebb

6 flood

Fig. 40

Full rudder in a modern auxiliary cruiser under power. The slick shows that the diameter of this turn was only a little over the waterline length of the yacht. (Author's photo)

Headsail bagged on the stay. Sheets, halyard and tack are still attached because the sail was bagged to save it from becoming muddy when the anchor was raised soon after. (Author's photo)

TOP LEFT Slab reefing lines rove to second and third reef. Lines are external here, but internal lines with jamming levers at the boom gooseneck are now common. (*Yachting Monthly* photo)

TOP RIGHT The slab reef. Hooks on the boom allow loose sail to be tidied up by engaging loops of elastic shockcord while the main loads are confined to tack and clew. The even strain and good set of the sail can be seen. (*Yachting Monthly* photo)

LEFT An improvised tack hook on a slab reef. It is important to haul down the tack as close to the gooseneck as possible otherwise the sail will set poorly with wrinkles around the tack area. (*Yachting Monthly* photo)

OPPOSITE PAGE Slab reef with rubber shockcord and hooks. The purpose is solely to tidy up the loose bunt of sail; the load is taken at tack and clew. (Author's photo)

TOP LEFT The Hood Sea Furl 2. The gear in the foreground is suitable for craft up to around 30 ft and it employs a continuous line lead to a winch by the cockpit. The bigger gear has a drum to contain the furling line.

RIGHT An outside-mast version of mainsail roller stowing, by Trevor Reed/Stearn and South Coast Rod Rigging. This arrangement is a close cousin to headsail rolling systems. There is also a much more sophisticated inside-mast design made by Hood Sails. (*Yachting Monthly* photos)

ABOVE Typical rafting-up situation. In such cases there is always a boat in the middle which has to be extricated because she wants to leave. Good reason for using your own lines. (Author's photo)

LEFT Anchor tripping line buoy improvised from a fender also indicates to other people that it is not a regular mooring – which they might pick up in error! (*Yachting Monthly* photo)

LEFT 'Potato patch' drag test on a Danforth anchor, although misleading in some respects, shows the great volume of soil displaced as it begins to dig. (*Yachting Monthly* photo)

ABOVE Three shots taken at one-minute intervals in wind against tide conditions. Some of the foreground boats are sheering around while others lie comparatively quietly.
(*Yachting Monthly* photo)

This combined samson post and chain snubber would be invaluable when getting the anchor in rough conditions. (*Yachting Monthly* photo)

Bitter-ending the cable on a short line allows it to be brought up on deck for slipping or for tailing on extra scope. (Author's photo)

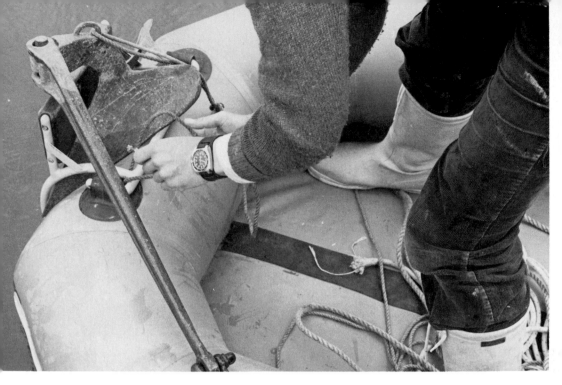

Carrying out a small kedge in an inflatable dinghy. The standard outboard motor bracket provides a good lodging for it. (*Yachting Monthly* photo)

The wind potential of a thunderstorm cannot be guessed. A yacht dragging anchor in such a squall might be in danger for only so long as it lasted – minutes, or half an hour. (*Yachting Monthly* photo)

The same coast from different distances and angles can appear very different indeed. The yacht from which the pictures were taken was moving from right to left and the dominence of the mound is lost against a new background as it begins to draw abeam. (*Yachting Monthly* photo)

A narrow angle converging course, whether bow to bow or with the larger faster ship overtaking the yacht, is always much harder to assess, particularly by night and when in the early stages of the situation the two vessels are some miles apart. The close quarters crossing situation in the second photo is plainly quite unacceptable, yet the same relative situation in terms of courses and speeds can begin with the two vessels a couple of miles or more apart. The need for constant checks by hand bearing compass is plain. (*Yachting Monthly* photo)

The man has been brought alongside, but what does the lone hand do now? A weak person could not get aboard unaided and the narrow side deck precludes useful help from on board. (*Yachting Monthly* photo)

Getting a man aboard in the mainsail. In average conditions this could save a life, but to attempt it in a high wind and sea would probably waste precious time unless the yacht was well manned. A line around the victim's chest is essential, to keep him attached to the boat, and it can then be led forward to help pull him into the bight of the sail and hold him there against sliding down out of it. (*Yachting Monthly* photo)

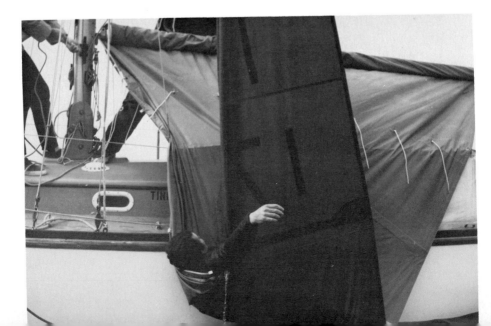

ABOVE This simple peg release on my own boat is effective and almost of nil cost. Both guardwires have pegs and the pegs are joined by a tug-line. The upper peg also holds the corner of the spray dodger so that wires and dodger can be freed for action with a single sharp tug. (Author's photo)

LEFT High modern topsides add to the problem of recovering a person from the water. This ladder was made from driftwood and the double loop allows the weighted bottom step to be lowered under water. Another possibility is a couple of small tyre fenders hung one above the other (open side outwards) with the lower tyre partly submerged to provide an armhold or step. More comfortable and stable than a bight of rope. (Author's photo)

The value of light-reflective tape, in this case Scotchlite manufactured by 3-M, is brought out dramatically in these unretouched photos. The self-adhesive tape can be applied to lifejackets, buoys, rafts and even individual sailing smocks. With a powerful torch aboard the yacht the reflection is brilliant, and more reliable than many of the dry battery powered life-lights.

ABOVE It is seldom realized that one of the biggest problems involved in fire at sea is the density of smoke, particularly in the case of fibreglass (GRP) boats. Once GRP is really alight it burns with great heat and if initial attempts to put out the fire don't succeed the boat is almost certainly going to burn out – unless outside help is available. (Carel Toms photo)

LEFT An emergency in the making. The halyard on the port side of the mast has come adrift. If not noticed it may well go overboard and should there be a need for engine power in a hurry the consequences can be guessed. The tidy coiling and stowing of all loose lines has a good deal of sense in it. (*Yachting Monthly* photo)

Visibility perhaps half a mile but the possibility of thicker banks must be allowed for. This ship could vanish again before you could look round. (Author's photo)

Visibility 100 yards? In fog it is wise to keep trying to estimate just how far you can see because fog can thicken from several hundred yards visibility to less than one hundred without a crew being aware of it. (*Yachting Monthly* photo)

ABOVE Flaring bows would strike a yacht's mast before her hull could be hurled aside by the bow wave – if she was that lucky. The ship could easily be travelling at this speed in fog. (Author's photo.)

RIGHT An attempt at contriving a jury rudder. It seems very unlikely that these lashings will hold for long. Securing an improvised rudder blade to a pole or spar is a big problem and a little advance planning in the form of G-cramps or locker lids specially adapted for this use would be time well spent because of all the emergencies the loss of a rudder at sea is one of the most common. (*Yachting Monthly* photo)

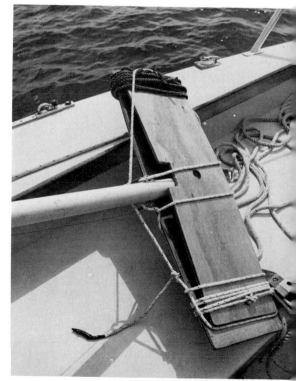

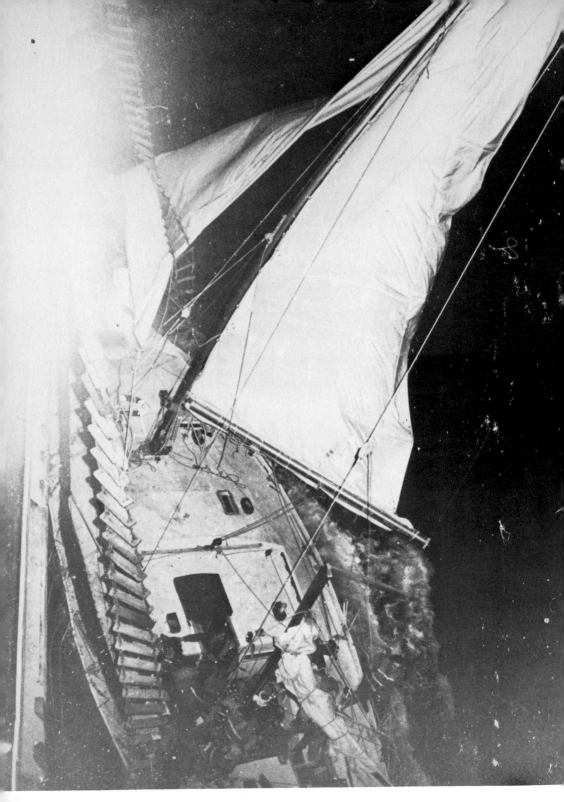

Rescue of a yacht's crew by a big ship almost always results in heavy damage to the yacht if the vessels lie alongside and in rough weather it is even more hazardous. In this print and despite its poor quality the wildly swaying pilot ladders can be seen. Later, survivors in attempting to climb these ladders were swept off and never seen again. (Photo source unknown)

Should it be necessary to cope with these conditions under sail alone (fuel shortage, fouled propeller, engine trouble or sail purism) it is better to take a sheet of tracing paper and plot the many shifts and short distances on any conveniently large scale. For instance, a unit of 1 inch = 1 nautical mile using a tenths ruler works well. A right-angle grid cross is drawn on the paper, which can then be laid over the chart compass rose for setting off the various headings. Distances in nautical miles (n.m.) and tenths are set off, using the 1 inch unit, and the sheet is re-centred on the compass rose for each new heading. Finally the grid centre is placed over the rose again and the distance in mile units and direction of the last mark is measured. The operation can be carried out twice, once for tidal movements and again for yacht headings and distances (Fig. 41).

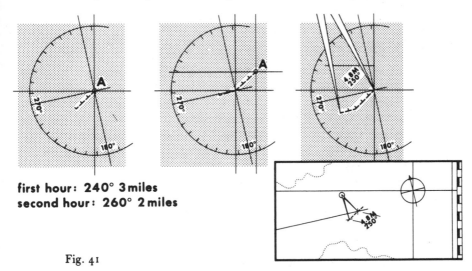

first hour: 240° 3 miles
second hour: 260° 2 miles

Fig. 41

SENSE OF POSITION

A navigator working the narrow seas develops a sense of position. He becomes aware of the direction and distance of land, islands or marks relative to his own changing position. When we are teaching blind students to sail and to cruise at sea, one of the essentials is that they are 'shown' on their tactile chartlets where they are and how the land lies. This sense of orientation is important.

Disorientation is equally important to avoid. A watchkeeper having been woken for his watch and coming on deck on a dark night is totally disorientated at first. Only the lighted compass gives him a sense of heading, then comes the angle of wind to course, then he becomes aware of any lights visible and where and what they are. Finally he is orientated: his sense of position is complete and he has a mental map of ship relative to surroundings. It is important that all watchkeepers should be orientated;

those going on should be briefed by the off-going watch as soon as the former have woken up properly.

A light following breeze for instance, which can hardly be felt, deprives us of one signpost. An accidental deviation from course in handing over the helm may bring a light from ahead to a point on the bow and a second light appears ahead; he steers for it and if the course has not been given clearly trouble ensues. Quick changes of course made in an emergency can totally disorient the helmsman on a very dark night. I was once on a race which had the Wolf Rock lighthouse as a turning mark. We had a panic getting the spinnaker down and by the time we came on the wind for the next leg none of us including the navigator could be certain that we had actually rounded the rock. It seems impossible but we were all totally disorientated.

NIGHT PILOTAGE

While accepting that positive identification of lights is far easier at night, various other factors have to be reckoned with. It is not natural to the average person to be fully alert and active at 2 a.m. when the body feels that it should be asleep. Distances are deceptive because we have no ready means of comparison; in daylight a headland looming close due to its height suddenly assumes its proper distance when we distinguish the size of a row of cottages. A distant bright light may look weaker than a nearer but dimmer light. Speed and wind strength are also deceptive, both seeming greater at night. At night also the coastline looks closer than it actually is, and in the event that there are hazards within a mile or so of known ones in known positions, there is an eerie sense of dangerous proximity not present by daylight.

The navigator has to be aware of and allow for all these curious factors. The character of lights must also be understood. Not just their mechanical characteristics – flashing, occulting or whatever – but their appearance over the water. A distant powerful lighthouse or lightship projects a 'loom' long before the actual light becomes visible and especially when low cloud is present. Then the beam can be seen, wheeling up from below the horizon, and in due course the pin-point of the actual light as it comes up into line of sight. By knowing its elevation and the height of our own eye the Lights Seen Dipping tables give a useful distance off.

It is when closer that the distance from a light becomes deceptive. With lighthouse or lightship the searchlight beam panning over open water begins to throw a reflection, in calm conditions visible for 3–4 miles and less in broken water. In time the beam picks out the yacht's sails and by then we are inside the 1 mile circle. The light touching the yacht is clear evidence that we are too close, should there be off-lying dangers. Naturally the effect depends very much on the clarity of the night and the strength of the particular light.

The twinkle on the water from a lit buoy again betrays its close proximity. The strings of seafront lights ashore seen dipping or in reflection, the loom of distant towns and ports and the lights of big vessels all alter character with distance and atmospheric conditions; an aura around the lights of a ship can be an early warning of fog or mist.

The arch problem when piloting by eye at night is that although lit buoys can be identified precisely by their light characteristics, it is harder to visualise the general lie or pattern of a group of buoys. By day we can see anything within our circle of visibility, note their relative positions and relate them to the chart. At night their lights go on and off in a confusing lack of order and other buoys well outside our daytime circle of visibility but pricking our horizon by reason of their height, add to the confusion. We can find ourselves surrounded by a mass of flashing, winking and occulting lights, none of which make any sense at all – at first.

If worried, heave-to or at any rate slow right down. Keep calm. Pick a couple of buoys and time them carefully, then go below and find them on the chart. Choose a couple which are either flashing continuously or are in some way distinctive. Take careful bearings and plot them. They may not give a good fix but they provide a 'handhold' of orientation and other lights relative to them then fall into position. Not until you have slotted your own ship's position into the pattern and identified the buoys which are important to your course should you draw sheets and proceed. There may be a score of lights around you, but probably only four of them are of immediate concern: stick to those and ignore the others unless they look like providing a useful transit.

Never accept a mystery. It is very easy to explain a mystery by blaming it on a buoy being withdrawn or changed at short notice by a sloppy 'foreign' lights authority – and it can happen – but unless you know exactly where you are by other means don't *assume* anything.

EXERCISE 1   Finding Transits

Demonstrate near and distant transits as follows. Upraised thumb at arm's length in line with the most distant object in the room; move the head a few inches from side to side. Thumb within a foot of your eyes; move the head a similar amount. Notice the extent of the thumb's 'jump' in each case. The closer you are to the front object of the pair the more rapidly the transit opens and closes. Two distant objects which are close together give an unreliable transit.

When next at sea and following the coast or buoyage, practice plotting entirely by transits (assuming you're in safe water). Buoys, beacons, houses, churches, headlands etc.

EXERCISE 2 Pilotage in fog

Select a simple triangular course around buoys in open water. Failing this a 2 mile leg offshore and back to the starting place. The aim is for the navigator to remain below at the chart, resisting the temptation to look out. Using all available aids he must plot and order courses to steer. Crew are allowed to inform him of necessary temporary changes of course; they can 'sight' buoys etc at a range of 200 yards. The aim is to monitor blind pilotage ability and to analyse errors made. This exercise is great fun and one of the most valuable training exercises one can do.

EXERCISE 3 Buoyage orientation

Set out on the table top a collection of small, different objects (thimble, pea, matchbox etc) in a square. With the eye at table level view the group from a variety of angles and note how the various objects alter their relative positions. Get a friend to test you: while you are not looking he makes a series of eye-level sketches from different viewpoints (Fig. 42). You must quickly orient yourself from each in turn.

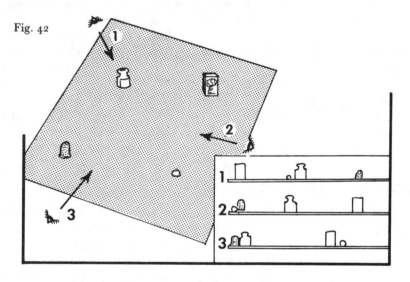

Fig. 42

At sea. Check your height of eye and distance to horizon from almanac tables. Select a buoy or mark soon to be passed and strike a horizon circle around it (e.g. radius 3.8 miles or whatever). Upon arriving at that spot note what you can see of distant marks etc both inside and outside the circle. Continue sailing, drawing fresh circles as you go. Note what details can be seen, the point at which objects begin to dip, the effect of sunlight and shadow, or uniform greyness, on distant objects. Note the relationship of buoys to each other in terms of angle and distance.

EXERCISE 4   Reliability of bearings

On a day when there is a bit of a jump, ask crew members to take a set of three bearings (the same set), each in turn. Plot these and note the discrepancies. Repeat the exercise when on the mooring and at rest; don't let the figures be known until all have completed the set.

EXERCISE 5   Tidal set

Lay a course across a tidal stream, preferably in an estuary, and calculate the rate from the tidal atlas. Apply a correction, steer it and note the outcome. Estimate the extent of any error as closely as possible and account for it.

EXERCISE 6   Accuracy of three-point compass fix

Take your hand bearing compass with you on a winter walk. Using an Ordnance Survey or other topographical map (6 inch = 1 mile makes it more interesting) try to fix your exact position from available precise landmarks. Variation is shown on all maps. It is best to take a series of different three-point fixes and mark visually on the map exactly where you are standing for each set. Work out the bearings and plot them when you get home. This exercise may indicate a need to have your compass checked; it will also be an indication of the accuracy you can expect at sea, taking bearings from a moving platform.

CHAPTER VIII
The Skipper

Situations

1 It has been a hard passage but the lights of the destination can be seen. The skipper views them with mixed feelings, though; his crew long for rest and comfort but he is very uncertain about that rock-bound approach and entrance.

2 Four hours out and the lively head sea has taken its toll. The skipper looks around at his suffering family. 'We're supposed to be here for pleasure,' he reflects. 'O.K. we'll alter course and make for an easier, nearer goal. We can always tackle the longer hop later.'

3 'Right,' says the skipper, 'go ashore and enjoy the local fete by all means but don't forget that we're sailing at 3 a.m. The tide waits for no man least of all men with a hangover.'

In a family cruiser the skipper is the father of the family and he transfers his role as father and husband from life ashore to the life afloat. If he is easygoing ashore he cannot easily alter his attitude when afloat. If he attempts to show a sterner front it is put down to bad temper. The kids are uncertain and his wife begins to wonder what he is worrying about. He knows that his orders must be obeyed, that there should be a firmer discipline, but he doesn't know how to impose it and his wife is both worried about his uncertainty and losing confidence in him. She covers up her own uncertainty by beginning to nag.

The same man with the same uncertainties but crewed by 'some of the lads from the club' might react very differently. His crew is as proficient as he is, perhaps more. He is aware of this and he knows better than to try bluffing them with science as he does with his family; to attempt to discipline his mates would be asking for good-humoured ridicule. More likely than not he accepts a purely titular role as skipper and bows to the advice of his peers. Perhaps this is an altogether too simplistic picture but it serves to illustrate some of the tensions at work. It is by no means easy to be a good, let alone a competent, skipper in a small cruising yacht.

Easy-going or lax, artificially strict or subservient to his crew, none of these traits are desirable. The skipper of a crew consisting of friends or family has a difficult job in striking the right balance. He must acknowledge that some members have skills and knowledge superior to his own, and use them rather than resent them. He is a sort of chairman with a casting vote who listens, analyses and controls, maintaining direction and making the final decisions. Many decisions will be made at leisure; others must be instant ones, to be obeyed instantly in a crisis. These may be instinctive decisions and hopefully the right ones. It is a measure of the good skipper's personality that a crew will support the outcome however it turns out. He is responsible for the safety and the pleasure of his crew and they are responsible in their support. It is the unpopular but necessary decisions made and accepted which reveal how well a crew are in tune.

A merchant ship, trawler, warship or racing yacht all have a purpose and a goal be it carrying cargo from A to B or completing a course in competition. Having a definite goal makes a skipper's job easier because however nasty the going, however tired and wet the crew, there is a sense of purpose which relieves the skipper of the decision to go on or go back. In a family cruising yacht there is often no good reason why the discomfort should be prolonged, why one port isn't as good as the next but easier to reach. The only purpose is pleasure and a loosely structured schedule or cruising plan. Occasionally there are navigational or other requirements that dictate carrying on in the face of discomfort, but often, much more often, the decision falls squarely into the skipper's lap and a committee decision or a general vote will not help. If the outcome to such a vote is favourable the crew congratulate themselves and if it is unfavourable they blame the skipper for being indecisive.

A skipper must identify the general objective – a number of days spent cruising in a certain area with the maximum possible pleasure – and he must draw a clear line between this objective and his responsibility for safety and general good. He has to evaluate what his ship and crew are capable of doing. With a crack racing crew and a good fast boat crew exhaustion is a far smaller factor than it is with a family crew. He must also know his own limitations in terms of skill, knowledge, stamina and what he should *not* attempt.

There is a great temptation to talk over every problem with his crew and this is fair enough, but he must admit to himself why he wants to do so. A broad choice of ideas can only be good; it may also be a secret desire for support, for approval and a sharing of the possible blame. It is one thing to think out the options and lay them before his crew for their opinion before making up his mind finally and yet another thing to say, in effect, 'What would you *like* me to do?' You cannot pass the buck and be a trusted skipper.

The classic example is that of deciding whether or not to sail when the wind is strong but other boats are going out. The usual way out of this dilemma is to 'go out and have a look at it.' If it is truly dirty outside the yacht can return with crew doubts settled. What one yacht and crew can tackle is by no means a reason for taking a very different crew to sea. All too often, though, the decision is less easy to make. The yacht could take it but could the crew? Conditions might get just a little worse and discomfort might become danger. The course might be downwind and apparently innocuous unless for some reason the yacht had to be turned upwind. Unless she can be handled on any point of sailing in a particular weight of wind a yacht cannot be said to be under control.

We'll suppose that this yacht went out and the skipper decided that she could cope with a 10 mile beat to a headland, after which they would be in easier reaching conditions. After an hour of hard, wet going half the crew have had enough and all they want is to get into quiet water. There is a haven abeam but it means a reach up a long river. Most of the crew welcome the diversion; it seems a good compromise. Within half an hour the wind eases and the sky clears. What should the skipper do? Carry on and maybe spend a hot peaceful day impatient to resume the cruise, or return to the original course? He does the latter but in spite of using the engine the wind goes lighter and the tide turns foul just before they reach the headland. It begins to drizzle.

Disaffection at once. Some argue that they should never have deviated, others wish they had reached that haven and the comfort of a cosy pub ashore. The skipper resents the criticism, feels inadequate and vows to keep 'this lot' at sea until the destination is reached. Pigheaded obstinacy replaces the wish to do the best by his crew.

Safety was not an issue. He should have weighed up the odds more carefully and laid the facts on the line for his crew right at the beginning. *For going on:* the ship was sound and the crew capable of the effort, there was no forseeable danger and the objective was worthwhile. *Against:* discomfort and some seasickness for a limited period. 'If we go to sea it will be horrible', he might have said. 'If we go out we'll keep going unless there is some unforseen trouble and we have to turn back. What do you want to do?'

The passage that is commenced and then given up on a committee decision in order to 'have another go tomorrow' is another enigma. If it is patently obvious that it is inviting trouble to press on, the decision is easy and defendable; but it may very well be nothing more than wet discomfort again. Is the ship and crew good enough? Is the weather pattern stable? Is the objective worthwhile? Committee decisions are usually bad news: if the outcome proves to be a good one the crew congratulate themselves but if it turns out to be the wrong one they condemn the skipper for lack of conviction. There is one vital factor to consider in the case of a family crew, though. Too many uncomfortable passages create a dread of going to sea and no objective is worth that!

The crew has the responsibility to create an atmosphere in which the skipper is free to weigh up the odds dispassionately and make *pure* decisions. If he is made to fear condemnation of his occasional wrong decisions; if he stands in line for a nagging for every spell of discomfort his decisions bring about; then his decisions will be biased. Sooner or later he will turn round and run into real danger in an effort to bring his critics to the shelter they demand.

I have a personal system for resolving this sort of decision: it works for me and it may work for you. Faced with a go in or stay out decision or any decision involving danger, I imagine myself standing before a Magistrate being asked to explain how I came to wreck my command.

Magistrate: 'Were you conversant with the river approaches?'

Me: 'I thought the pilotage would become plain once we were closer in.'

Magistrate: 'Did you consider that there was danger involved in attempting an unknown river at night and in poor conditions?'

Me: 'Yes, but I . . . .'

Magistrate: 'Could you not have remained hove-to offshore until daylight in perfect safety?'

Me: 'Yes I could have done that, but . . . '

Magistrate: 'You must have had a very good reason to take such a risk when there was a perfectly safe alternative. What was your reason please?'

Me: 'The rest of the crew were getting fed up and tired . . .'

Most decisions are go or stay decisions. The need to get back in time for work on Monday morning. A rendezvous with friends at the next port. Holiday time running out fast and only half the planned cruise accomplished. A delivery trip planned for the only weekend convenient. A decision to sail based on inadequate weather information and so forth. It is important for the skipper to do all his thinking privately, exploring all the consequences, and only when he has done this to lay the facts before the crew. He can discuss at length; other opinions are valuable. Having made the decision he must then stick by it, unless some quite new and important factor emerges.

There is only one skipper to each boat.

LEARNING

The more we know about the subject the easier it is to make fast, correct decisions. We will never learn it all, though; we will continue to make mistakes for the rest of our sailing careers. The lucky people are those who serve their apprenticship on the deck of an experienced skipper and *then* tackle the classroom aspects. This way they learn good habits first. A great many people have no choice. The evening classes and the books happen first and the practical stuff later. The real drawback is that one learns the 'school solution' in advance of its practical application, and all too often people develop a sort of awe, a reluctance to seek a commonsense solution because they feel that there must be a textbook answer to every situation.

I heard of a beginner adrift on a fast ebb through dense moorings, no engine, no room to anchor. He was aware that a professional or an experienced yachtsman would have known the proper thing to do: he did not. He thought fast. Either his boat was going to come into violent and expensive contact with one of the moored yachts or he could settle for lesser damage. He very quickly turned out a light kedge, bent on a line, and as he was swept close by the cockpit of a moored yacht he flung his kedge aboard her. It did about five pounds worth of damage and brought him up safely astern.

Reading, reading, reading. It doesn't much matter whether a book deals with a passage in the Tasman Sea or how to bleed a diesel fuel line. You may only remember a fraction of it but that fraction may well become vital someday. I know of at least three yachtsmen who are alive today because each recalled, during an emergency, some scrap of information once read. One was a case of dismasting, another was a man overboard crisis and the third fought a fire.

Keeping out of trouble is very largely a matter of thinking ahead. A chess mentality. Thinking ahead not only in terms of passage planning but in the small things. Anticipating trouble before it happens. The crew who bends over the engine to start it while wearing a necktie forgets the flywheel. The winch handle left in the mast winch (just for a moment). The mainsheet not coiled ready for a fast gybe, and so on. Experience teaches this sort of awareness but it can be cultivated by habit too. One can mull over things quietly. What would I do, *now*, if the engine suddenly stopped? How might I set about rigging a jury rudder? Suppose the weather cuts up nasty once we've turned the headland and brought the reefs under our lee? This sort of thinking isn't morbidity – it's far too constructive for that.

EXERCISE 1

When anything goes wrong it sets off a chain reaction. Try this quiz, working back and forth between PORT and STARBOARD lists. Add up your score and read the summary. Try it again choosing different options and see what they lead to.

PORT LIST

1. It is dark. You are moored in mid-river, it's half-ebb and you are rowing out with a friend and already down-tide when an oar breaks. Would you?
a Use the oars as paddles and try to work back upstream to the yacht?
b Row with one oar and steer with the broken one?
c Paddle back to shore despite being set far downstream?
If *a* turn to STARBOARD 1. If *b* STARBOARD 2. If *c* STARBOARD 3.
2. You are drifting in the dinghy, your friend stands up and falls over-

board. Would you:

a Balance while he climbs in over the side?

b Over the stern?

c Over the bow?

If *a* turn to STARBOARD 4. If *b* STARBOARD 5. If *c* STARBOARD 4.

3. Finally on board. In the morning, head to wind and tide you start the engine, let go the mooring and move ahead, fouling the buoy rope around the propeller. Moments later you are lying stern-on to wind and tide moored by the propeller, the engine now stalled. Would you:

a Let go anchor, cut the rope and swing free?

b Try to hook the mooring from the stern, get a line on it and take it round to the bows?

c Set a headsail and cut the buoy rope adrift?

If *a* see STARBOARD 6. If *b* see STARBOARD 7. If *c* see STARBOARD 8.

4. Unlikely to work but an obvious first move. See choice *b*.

5. Sensible decision. Move to PORT 8.

6. You are sailing without engine or anchor. Luckily neither are required and you win your way back to your still fouled anchor. Would you:

a Consider that because it is so firmly held it is therefore safe enough to lie on overnight?

b Try for a tow into a marina berth until morning, when the mooring can be put to rights and your anchor recovered?

c Sleep on board, on the fouled anchor, with a view to enlisting some help next day?

If *a* see STARBOARD 9. If *b* see STARBOARD 10. If *c* see STARBOARD 11.

7. Unlikely to work. Turn to PORT 9, deciding to manage without an engine.

8. You may now turn to PORT 9.

9. You run aground, losing the dinghy, engine out of action and the tide ebbing. The wind is blowing *off* the shoal you have grounded on. Would you:

a Relax, make tea and wait until the tide floods.

b Set the jib quickly and back it, trying to heel her at the same time (fin-keel hull)?

c Throw the anchor out astern and try heaving from the bows?

If *a* see STARBOARD 12. If *b* see STARBOARD 13. If *c* see STARBOARD 14.

10. Not satisfactory seamanship but you'll be safe. Now add your score.

11. Your life is not in danger. You could have chosen STARBOARD 14 *a* or *c*. You will get a fat salvage claim made against you. Now add your score.

12. A seamanlike gamble and the odds are that it will come off – a carefully calculated risk. See summary. Add your score.

13. You may now tackle STARBOARD 14.

STARBOARD LIST

1. The tide is too strong, you should have chosen PORT 1*c*. Turn to PORT 2.
2. It wouldn't work. You should have chosen PORT 1*c*. You now lose the broken oar. Would you:
a Signal for help and yell?
b Try to scull over the stern although there is no provision there for this?
c Paddle one side, using a canoe stroke, and make for the nearest shore?
If *a* see PORT 2. If *b* see PORT 2. If *c* see PORT 3.
3. Correct answer, turn to PORT 3.
*4. Wrong. You are now both in the water. Would you:
a Swim away to get help?
b Hang on and kick to keep warm?
c Hang on, shout, and hope to be swept close enough to be able to grab a moored vessel?
If *a* or *b* see PORT footnote. Meanwhile follow choice *c*. If *c* see PORT 3.
5. Correct. See PORT 3.
6. Your mooring is lost and your anchor now fouls the ground chain of the mooring on the seabed. Would you:
a Haul in the anchor in an attempt to raise and clear the ground chain?
b Resign yourself to a long wait until low water and then try?
c Slip and buoy your anchor so that you can at least go for a little sail, then use the fouled anchor as a mooring when you return?
If *a* see PORT 4. If *b* see PORT 5. If *c* see PORT 6.
7. Correct. You passed a bight around it from the dinghy and hauled it up from the stern. Then you got up some slack and made a line fast with a rolling hitch to the chain, leading it forward to your bow. You cut the buoy rope, replaced the buoy and rope on the chain and your mooring was saved. You must now attend to the fouled propeller. Would you:
a Hope to find the rope's end and pull while turning the propeller shaft in reverse?
b Secure the rope's end and start the engine (out of gear) then slam it in reverse?
c Tackle it the hard way, stripped off, over the side and trying to cut off the jammed turns with a saw-edged knife?
If *a* see PORT 7. If *b* see PORT 7. If *c* see PORT 8.
8. You are now careering downwind, down-tide with no engine and no mooring to return to. Turn to PORT 9.
9. The anchor came free on the turn of tide and dragged. Your boat was wrecked. You should have chosen PORT 6*b*.
10. Safest. Now turn to PORT 9.

Footnote to STARBOARD 4.
Usually dangerously wrong, as explained in the summary.

11. During the night you begin to drag when the anchor breaks free of the mooring. Would you:

a Pay out more cable until it holds?

b Set sail, haul in the anchor and go in search of a mooring?

c Send up a distress flare to summon help?

If a see PORT 13. If b see PORT 9. If c see PORT 9.

12. Probably easiest but should have tried PORT 9b. Try STARBOARD 14.

13. You may now proceed to STARBOARD 14.

14. While aground an onshore gale develops. The tide is still well out but flooding. Would you:

a Let go the anchor, haul out plenty of chain, then leave the boat and walk a mile ashore over the sands?

b Send up distress rockets?

c Walk your anchor out to full scope seawards, reef in readiness and then wait for her to float, trusting in the flatness of the shore?

If a see PORT 10. If b see PORT 11. If c see PORT 12.

SCORING

Score 10 points for every correct answer, 5 for every other answer. Correct answers are:

PORT	STARBOARD	
1C	2C	
2B	4C	(deduct 2 for every PORT and STARBOARD number
3B	6B	you have to refer to)
6B	7C	
9B	11A	
	14C	

If your score after deductions is: 45 or over = Very Good, 35–45 = Passable, 20–35 = Weak on Seamanship.

SUMMARY

PORT 1   Fighting the current would be useless unless it was very weak. Rowing with one oar and steering with the broken bit is impracticable as it would be impossible to pull hard enough on the good oar without spinning the dinghy. Returning to the shore downstream the only safe alternative.

PORT 2   Re-entry over the stern is the only safe method unless the dinghy is an inflatable (I didn't say it was).

PORT 3   By working along the mooring chain for a distance (assuming there is slack enough) a line might be made fast and the load taken to the bow: the best answer if possible. Other methods could have been considered provided there was a line made fast to the chain prior to cutting adrift from the fouled buoy.

PORT 6   A fouled anchor is always suspect in terms of hold. If it dislodges on the next swing of tide and leaves the yacht on a shortened scope she must drag.

PORT 9   As the wind is off the shoal there is a narrow chance that fast work with a backed jib and heeling the yacht over might get her off. With an onshore breeze there is nothing to be done. An anchor let go from the stern and hauled at from the bow just wouldn't work.

STARBOARD 2   Yelling and waving at night is a waste of time unless somebody else is nearby. Try paddling canoe fashion by sitting right aft, weight to one side to list the boat. The stroke is J-shaped with a twist of the blade towards you prior to leaving the water, which counteracts the tendency to turn the boat which is a consequence of paddling on one side.

STARBOARD 4   Much depends on the *known* distance to shore and the strength of the swimmer but the laid down RULES insist that one should never leave the boat. Many drownings have occurred through doing so. Kicking or exercising to keep warm is a dangerous fallacy. It hastens deep chill and hypothermia. Conserve energy and lash yourself to the boat.

STARBOARD 6   It would be impossible to lift a heavy mooring ground chain without special gear. It might just be worth trying at low tide, rigging a tackle aloft. Unless one has a second anchor aboard it is folly to be under way without an anchor.

STARBOARD 7   If a rope fouls badly enough to stall the engine, the rope turns will be as hard as iron on the shaft. Tugging the free end *can* work if it can be led straight aft *between* the propeller blades so that they turn and unwind the rope when the shaft is reversed by hand. If it can't be done, going overboard is the only answer. Beware chill. Use a hacksaw; a sharp knife won't touch those packed-solid fibres. The engine in reverse would never work; it might also be damaged.

STARBOARD 11   If an anchor only needs more scope in order to make it hold, why not give it some? Careering around in the dark looking for a vacant mooring is inviting more trouble. Distress signals when nobody is really in distress are stupid and selfish.

STARBOARD 14   This is one of those arguable questions. If the man had his family aboard or if his own life would plainly be endangered, he would be wise to anchor the boat on full scope and leave her. Note the remark about the flatness of the shore. A truly flat shore ensures that a boat of moderate draft will float well before the water is deep enough for waves to become big enough to damage her by pounding. Since the shore was flat, the owner who waited for the tide stood a very good chance of being able to sail her off or at least signal for a tow.

CHAPTER IX
The Night Watch

Situations

1 'Shall we call the skipper or let him sleep on a bit longer?' the crew say, eyeing the exhausted and deeply slumbering man with compassion. Meanwhile the wind falls still lighter and speed drops to barely steerage way.

2 'Skipper, skipper.'
'Um . . . Yes, what is it then?' He listens sourly to the news that Berry Head is abeam 10 miles inshore. He hadn't wanted to be told, it was not important to his navigational strategy, he'd been woken up for nothing.

3 'Where's Jack?'
'In the heads, lying down again, I don't know. He's pretty useless if you ask me.'

The planning of a night watch system is aimed at maintaining an alert and functional section of the crew in command of the deck from dusk until dawn. It is more important to concentrate on the low-ebb period of the night and man it adequately than to arrange an even spacing of crew power throughout the whole night. First, though, we must take a good look at the material we have available.

A strong crew need not be numerically strong. Two experienced people well used to night watches may be far stronger than three times the number of inexperienced people. Or a one-man watch with wind vane self-steering, provided it's an old hand and knows how to stay awake. Manual steering doesn't help a really tired person to stay alert. In fact the lighted compass bowl has a highly hypnotic effect, especially on a very dark night.

The difficult period is from midnight until dawn. Most of us are quite used to staying up until 11.30 or later; then it is time for sleep and the fight begins. There is a good argument for doing a one-man stint from about dusk until midnight, then doubling up or shortening watches for the remainder of the night. An autopilot or vane steering gear is a valuable piece of night sailing gear after midnight because it allows people to move around, make hot drinks at frequent intervals, look at the chart, enter the logbook up, and all the other little jobs so vital to staying awake.

The course also has a strong influence on the arrangement of watches. The skipper/navigator may need to be on deck at a certain time when the yacht is due to cross a shipping lane or reach some critical point. The night watches must be built around this need in a small crew, otherwise it may mean that he is no sooner asleep than he is called: then he will get little if any rest for the remainder of the night.

Sleep is like the power in a battery. It can run only so long without being recharged, and the recharging is a vital part of passage planning.

A typical short sea passage of 20–30 hours, provided it is not un-expectedly extended to double that time, is no real problem for a healthy person. A twenty-four hour period without any sleep is tiring but not dangerously exhausting. Nobody will get much sleep even when off watch because they are not yet really tired. The urge to sleep which hits them in the small hours on watch is very largely a habit response. What is important is that people should rest and sleep if they can, which means a strict adherence to watch times. It isn't always remembered that the watch system has two respects: maintaining a deck strength and providing a chance for rest.

A watch system is a twenty-four hour thing; to set night watches only won't work. People have to be able to go below with a clear conscience knowing that they are officially 'off'. In a small cruiser crewed by a family this isn't easy because if the weather is pleasant everybody will be in the cockpit all day long instead of getting their batteries charged ready for night. With maybe two adults and one teenager plus a couple of ten-year-olds, the adults may divide the daytime into two six-hour watches and do three-hour spells during darkness with the teenager doubling up for the graveyard watches. Much depends upon the weather, though; one of my dearest memories is doing a whole night from dusk until dawn with a full moon and a perfect broad-reaching breeze. On a cold wet night two hours on watch is more than enough.

One very important thing is almost always forgotten by skippers who ship along friends with whom they have not sailed before – eyesight. A surprisingly large number of people suffer from colour blindness to a greater or lesser extent, maybe not even being much aware of it themselves. Where the reds and greens of shipping lights are concerned this can be serious. Also, strength of vision is taken for granted. Some people have very poor night vision or on a rainy night have the annoyance of wearing glasses which mist up constantly. It is quite possible to have a deck watch with a range of vision not extending more than half a mile, yet the watch below slumber on satisfied that the deck is well manned.

The watch on deck should have written orders to be followed. The course to steer, log entries to be made of distance run – on the hour (it keeps them awake), and lights or landmarks to look out for. Novices should be taught how to look for lights at sea; how to sweep the horizon slowly back and forth to allow the periphery of the eye, which is the part used in night vision, to pick up that first tiny gleam. The expression 'catching a glimpse from the corner of my eye' is physiological fact. The night watch should also be well briefed about emergencies.

Safety harness at night is an iron rule. In Situation 3 the whereabouts of Jack wasn't known, it was *supposed* that he had gone below. It was also possible that he had gone over the side. People do not always cry out when they fall overboard because the momentary shock renders them speechless. In a yacht moving at 6 knots their first cry will be a faint one well astern and unlikely to be heard.

Shipping watch is also an iron rule. Somebody must look all round the horizon at very frequent intervals. In busy waters every few minutes and in hazy weather a similar vigilance. They must also know how to interpret the lights of other ships; whether a ship is crossing, converging, or safely past. The rule should be that as soon as the coloured navigation lights of a ship are seen, wherever she may be, she must be kept under constant watch. Vessels may seem to be passing safely but who knows what course changes they may be about to make? Crew should also be required to check their boat's own lights regularly. They must also know that golden rule of calling the next watch with a hot drink five or ten minutes before the change. This isn't just kindness: some people take a long time to surface; they need time to gather their wits and take in the watch orders before being left in charge. The off-going watch hands over explicitly.

'We're about here' the new watch mate is told, on the chart. 'We had the loom of Beachy Head until half an hour ago but it is getting a bit murky, maybe rain on the way. We have a tanker or some-such safe to port and a small vessel, coaster maybe, dodging about inshore. Watch her.'

When to call the skipper is the subject of Situations 1 and 2. Unless he issues specific instructions to be woken at a particular time – for the shipping forecast, for a change of wind or speed, when a light is sighted, etc – it will be up to the crew. They must remember that *he is responsible*. If anything worries them, seems to threaten the ship in the slightest, he must be called. Even if he has only been asleep for half an hour he must be called. Every skipper encourages this: only by knowing that he will be called can he relax and sleep. It is a penance of his 'lofty' position that he will be called quite uneccessarily again and again. He must grit his teeth, thank his caller hollowly and bear it. I was once shaken violently awake by a novice who had been instructed to call me if 'anything at all' worried him. There was a plum stone blocking the heads!

At night certain provisions have to be made in advance. The watches should know where things they might need are to be found. They should have a good supply of things to chew such as nuts, dried fruit and so on;

this is morale-boost. Time crawls slowly. The thought that in another half hour I'll have another of those biscuits becomes very important, especially if alone. Then torches (note the plural), binoculars, bearing compass etc etc, all stowed handily. The little pocket or handbag torches are good because they don't produce more light than is needed on board and they are always in a pocket, provided they are handed over at change of watch.

There must be one very powerful light to be used as a means of drawing attention to the yacht should a ship seem to be shaping to pass uncomfortably close (call the skipper in good time unless competent to deal with this). There should be some form of low, soft lighting below decks, which safeguards precious night vision when light is needed below. The compass should have rheostat control so that it can be dimmed to a comfortable degree. There should also be a ready facility for brewing up tea or any other hot stimulant again and again. If Thermos flasks are used, it is far better to have about four small ones filled in advance than one big one because the constant opening and pouring will rapidly render the contents lukewarm.

Steering at night can be a delight or a purgatory. It is bad to become a slave to the compass bowl when a star can be found in the rigging (changed for another as often as necessary), and on a very dark night the roar of wind and water is an irresistable lullaby. The helmsman should be the best lookout. Apart from the arc hidden behind the headsail he has a clear forward view of the whole horizon; his mate should have the responsibility of watching astern and to leeward under the headsail.

A fast run in a quartering sea on a dark night is the worst, or most difficult, task of all and a navigator should allow a very large margin of windward error in his reckoning. It is very easy for a sleepy helmsman to become disorientated; he jerks awake with a guilty shock and it is then that he loses his place on the compass card and in panic applies the wrong helm.

Sudden alarm for any reason has an amazing effect upon sleepy people. They are instantly fully alert, but not necessarily thinking straight. The charge of adrenalin in the blood demands activity, and unco-ordinated activity leads to panic. For this reason even with a two-person watch one should be nominated as the person in charge. The aftermath of a minor panic is also a thing to acknowledge, being a sudden slump into even deeper lethargy.

A dark night makes one feel insecure. If the boat is moving fast there will be no need to tell people not to go roaming around the deck; the cockpit seems bleak enough in any case. At other times, though, be the night dark or moonlit, some people seem to like wandering around. It should be a golden rule that nobody should go forward on deck without good reason, that they should be hooked on before leaving the cockpit, and that their watchmate should keep them under observation the whole time. This is not an easy order to enforce in a big yacht but it is just as important. Men are especially vulnerable because they deem it their male prerogative to pee over the lee side rather than go below to the heads. An all-male watch can have a dinghy bailer kept handy in the cockpit; or they can use the loo like anybody else. I lost a very good friend this way. I was not with him but I heard the account later and how he went over the stern, despite having had one arm hooked around the backstay.

WATCH SYSTEMS

The traditional four on, four off two-watch plan with a couple of two-hour dog watches from 1600–1800–2000 takes a lot of beating on an extended passage because the dogs 'turn' the watch rotation and ensure that the hated 'graveyard watch' from midnight to 0400 doesn't always fall to the same people. On a short one or two night passage its value is debatable, and also when the crew consists of family, or a crew which is weak both numerically and in experience. It is then more important to ensure that the skipper/navigator gets adequate rest when he is able to and that the low-ebb hours are catered for.

The daytime six-hour system, 0600–1200–1800, allows the skipper ample sleeping time in morning or afternoon. Then, with a crew of four adults, two inexperienced, one moderately experienced, and the skipper who, while he may not be very experienced is nevertheless the one in charge, the dark hours can be divided up into shorter spells.

Until about 2100 the preparing, eating and clearing away of supper will keep the whole ship's company fairly occupied. Then from 2100 until midnight the mate or the skipper might keep a lone watch, this being the easy part of the night before sleepiness sets in and its inevitable chill. From midnight until 0300 the other more experienced hand takes over with one novice and is relieved by his opposite number with the other novice, who then finish the night and see the dawn in. These watches can be shortened to two-hour spells in uncomfortable weather.

There are many other systems. It is a matter for choice and for the particular needs of the moment. It is important that fairness is given full attention, though. People can become very easily niggled at 3 a.m. Life quickly becomes a simple matter of bed or no bed. The situation in which the whole system breaks down, leaving one or two people to do everything, is all too common.

SEASICKNESS

Because it is the worm in the apple, the secret dread, the weakness in an otherwise strong team, seasickness is a subject which could well merit a whole chapter to itself. There is apparently no such thing as being completely immune to motion sickness, except for some deaf people. Some people are rarely if ever sick at sea but somewhere there is a motion of some sort that can do the trick.

Most people know the root cause of seasickness and that it is centred in the inner ear. Many non-sufferers put the whole thing down to strength or weakness of willpower. Undoubtedly it has some bearing and to sit waiting to be sick is halfway to being so in fact, but animals are prone to motion sickness. Conversely, there are plenty of people who can be genuinely sick on a ship in dry-dock.

There are two other close relatives to motion sickness which can be allied to it. Excitement sickness, such as highly experienced racing men can suffer prior to a race start, and hunger sickness. Very often people who have spent some twenty-four hours being seasick overcome it without realizing the fact and wake up hungry, again without realizing it. They still feel ill, but it is food that they need despite their repugnance at the very thought of it.

For this reason alone the provisioning for a sea passage is very important. Whatever the fit members of the crew may be able to take, there should also be a totally bland but nourishing alternative for the queasy. Plain wheat biscuits, crackers, salted porridge, an apple, in fact anything that will start people wanting to eat. A greasy cold sausage or leg of chicken is perhaps the nadir of the manu.

The importance of seasickness to yacht efficiency is as vital to planning as the fitness of ship and gear. Within a few hours a well-manned yacht can become dangerously inefficient. The navigator yawns over his hasty and sketchy chartwork, the helmsman yawns over the compass, and the rest of the crew either sit slumped in the cockpit corner or dead to the world down below. In picking a crew it is far more important to choose at least one member who is rarely sick than to recruit youth and muscle. The experienced yachtsman who is prone to sickness can usually be relied on to keep it under control. Sick he may be but he never misses a watch. Just the same, he is not fully efficient.

Attitude is important. Matter-of-factness. Seasickness is nothing to be ashamed of or to laugh at; it just happens to some people and not to others. Some can heave up promptly and recover, at least temporarily, while others fight the spasms and continue to feel dreadful. One cannot disguise queasiness either: the sallow complexion, the shivering, yawning and lassitude. Neither can the sufferers be allowed to just opt out and die quietly below unless by general consent. Others feeling equally wretched but doing their best to carry on might also wish they could opt out. As a general rule people should be turned out for their watch, for the general good of morale, albeit to be sent off watch by the watch leader ten minutes later. The plain fact is that while a person may be glad enough to pocket his pride and opt out at sea, when the ship reaches port there will be a subtle change in the atmosphere, those who kept all their watches feeling strangely superior and those who didn't ashamed and resentful.

Having made that point, let it be understood very clearly that a seasick person on a night watch is at great risk and must be watched constantly. The sudden frantic lurch to the lee rail coinciding with a roll of the ship could have a tragic result. Safety harness was never so important.

The general advice regarding pills and preventives of one sort or another is to find the brand that suits you best and stick to it. Then, *keep taking it* and *at the prescribed intervals*. Dosage of regular sufferers can be started as much as forty-eight hours before sailing; at the least it should start six hours before. The common problem is drowsiness which allied to post-midnight sleepiness may make it physically impossible to stay awake. I have seen a young lad in a sail training ship hanging by his harness, feet dragging to and fro on the deck, and deeply asleep. In fact teenagers seem more likely to go off into one of these profound slumbers than full adults.

The use of a drug hitherto prescribed for Menier's disease (affecting the balance) and in safe use for many years for that purpose has brought new relief to yachtsmen. The success rate is around eighty per cent or higher. It had been known as a motion sickness remedy for a long while but not until two sailing doctors propounded its value in *Yachting Monthly* did yachtsmen begin to take interest. Marketed in the UK as Stugeron and available over the counter, it has certainly revolutionized sailing for hundreds if not thousands of offshore yachtsmen, myself included. I have literally forgotten what it was like to be seasick, my wife also. Perhaps one of the best things about this drug is that in most cases it does not induce drowsiness – a fact that was testified to me by a Concorde pilot and a cross-Channel ferry skipper.

EXERCISE 1   How good is your night vision?

If you are a motorist you will know whether or not you have any degree of colour blindness – or should do. Compare your perception of detail at night when driving on country roads on dipped headlights with the moments immediately after on-coming headlights pass. You can compare your ability to recover by asking friends to study the view down the garden from a darkened room; each can state whether he can see a particularly indistinct object. Put on the lights for one minute then darken the room and try again. Take note at night of distant house lights; how far off can you see ordinary lights? This has a useful bearing on distance judging at sea, at night.

EXERCISE 2   Watch organization

You are expecting to reach a shipping separation zone at 2 a.m. You have already had one night at sea. Plan watches for the following crews

* = degree of experience, S = degree of seasickness liable, (45) = age.

Man (55) **	Man (60) ****	Woman (50) **S
Man (23) SS	Woman (34) SSS	Man (55) ***
Woman (22) ****	Girl (12) SSS	Man (28) ****
Boy (14) S	Boy (11) *S	Girl (13) S

EXERCISE 3   Shipping at night

Use a red and a green pen or crayon to colour the lights in the illustration *before* studying it. Give yourself a full minute to study all the traffic situations before turning to the answer in the Appendix. Give this test to any crew member who may be chosen as a night watch leader.

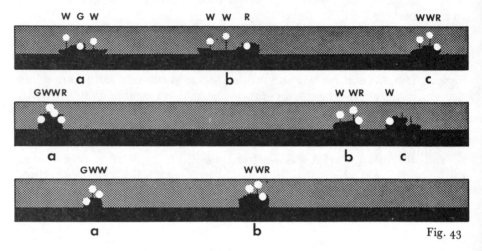

Fig. 43

CHAPTER X
Wind and Wave

Situations

1 The small sailing cruiser is hard on the wind at dusk, making poor progress. The nearest shelter is 15 miles ahead if she carries on. If she goes back she will be losing all the ground she has so painfully made. Nothing has actually gone wrong, but the crew are feeling the strain and everything below is soaking wet. . . . what should the skipper do for the best?

2 Running for safe shelter. The wind and sea are building up but the speed is exhilarating. She can get there before dusk if she keeps up the speed but there are no lights for night entry anyway. If she slows down she *won't* make it in daylight; moreover she will have a lee shore if it comes on to blow and the only shelter within reach will be an unlit river.

3 Coasting with a strengthening onshore wind and no safe harbours for the next 20 miles. To go back will mean coming hard on the wind to round a headland passed earlier and the tide will be foul. She is fine for so long as she is broad-reaching parallel to the coast but suppose the weather becomes really bad? The forecast hints at Force 7–8 and if she claws offshore now, they'll never find that river entrance in the worsening visibility.

Once a person begins going to sea in small boats he can never again be indifferent to the wind. When I was an infant my mother (with uncany foresight) used to urge me to sleep by telling me to 'Hush, listen to Mr Blow,' advice which has stuck with me for a lifetime. I was three years old then, but I have listened to Mr Blow with varying degrees of alarm and pleasure ever since.

To a sailing yachtsman the wind is the core of both pleasure and trouble. Without wind there would be no waves, other than tidal waves and such specialities as the Tsunami caused by submarine earthquake. If we study the wind we are halfway to becoming wise and competent seamen and women.

A chapter on potted meteorology in this book would be out of place. It is up to the reader to read up the subject elsewhere, from a text written by an expert specifically for small craft sailors. There are a number of them to be found, including *Meteorology at Sea* by Ray Sanderson, a marine forecaster and yachtsman. One cannot expect to become an expert, but by understanding the mechanics of weather one can make fuller use of broadcast reports and learn to anticipate a little.

One of the first realizations will be that the classic behaviour patterns of highs and lows – the progression from one type of weather to another as a low pressure front moves past – rarely seem to happen. Instead, and particularly in British waters, we get a hotch-potch of weather; cloud formations are rarely 'typical'. We have to sort out the scraggy remnants of a decayed front from the advance warnings of the next. In earlier times inshore seamen, fishermen and coasting traders, predicted weather by observing the signs around them and they were very good at it. What caught them out was the suddenly deepening low, the wave front, the secondary. They were concerned with very localized weather and baffled by anything that ran contrary to their experience. The huge depression building up its forces in mid-Atlantic was often outside their reckoning while the modern yachtsman can take it into account. We too are mainly concerned with short-term forecasts and local weather, but the wider picture is available to us. Shipping forecasts cover wide areas and predictions may hold good for one sector of an area but not for another. Coastal weather behaviour is much influenced by thermals and land masses and this too must be allowed for.

Yachtsmen are under one disadvantage compared to professionals: we are inclined to ignore the weather when we are not actually sailing whereas the professional is aware of it constantly. Weather is a non-stop performance. It moves from settled periods to unsettled; calms and high pressure spells to disturbed ones when depressions come sweeping in one after another. The only way we can develop a true understanding of it is to be aware of it day by day. This means listening to the early morning forecast before going to work, cocking an eye at the clouds while waiting for the train, noting the wind and temperature and during the day stealing an occasional look at the sky to see if the morning prediction is working out. By Friday evening, when we are turning our minds towards sailing, we are already aware of the trends past, present and predicated.

More often than not gale warnings don't seem to materialize. This is because the Met Office predicts a gale if it is likely; it may in any case hold true for elsewhere in that forecast area. What we must avoid is duping ourselves into believing that the Force 6 which we experience is a gale – simply because a gale was forecast. We must also avoid crying wolf. If a warning is out it must be heeded. Conversely, with no such warning given we may occasionally hit real trouble and winds approaching gale force but which are nothing more than a combination of a hot weather onshore thermal combined with an existing fresh (but no more than that) onshore breeze. The 'yachtsman's gale' which is a combination of a fresh breeze and a weather-going spring tide is another common deception, but none the less urgent for all that.

The ideal sailing breeze is Force 3–4. The seas which it raises are too small to much hinder a small cruiser of the average 25 to 30 ft and she can carry her genoa comfortably. She achieves her best passages under sail and her crew are happy and comfortable. In less wind she may have to motor a little if the crew are in a hurry, but if it is much stronger the problems begin to appear, dependant on whether she is on the wind or sailing free.

The lofty freeboard of today's boats offers splendid accommodation below but it doesn't always make for efficient windward sailing at sea. The trend towards motorsailer performance when a modest area of sail is beefed up by an engine run at low cruising revs is the acceptable answer. More important, though, in terms of making a windward passage at sea in a rising wind is not what the boat can do but what the crew can stand. Unless a crew is strong in either numbers or and stamina the hammer and slam of a small vessel being driven headlong into a rising sea will reduce it to a weak state of exhaustion within a very few hours. The average family crew can probably stand about four hours of it before the strain begins to tell – 10 miles dead to windward.

For the cruising family, then, a rising wind at sea sets a problem for the skipper. How much of this can my crew take? Can we reach sheltered water to windward before they tire? Is there shelter which I can reach and enter safely by altering to a more comfortable reaching course? Should we turn back now? Should we reduce sail, slow the boat right down and just keep plugging away or should we hang on, open up the engine and go bald-headed at it?

The crux of the matter is the future weather. If there is absolutely no reason to suppose that the existing weather is a foretaste of worse to come; if the barometer is steady and the forecast is reasonable you turn your collar up and keep going. We cannot turn tail for every little blow without becoming weather–shy. Sooner or later we will have to cope with really bad weather and every crew needs experience. If there is a real risk of a deterioration and winds rising to a gale or near-gale, it is a very different matter. A skipper with a vulnerable crew must at all costs avoid it if he can because a ship is only as strong as her crew.

Ideally every skipper should have had gale experience. If it is at all possible the best plan is to get in a season's crewing in offshore racing, but without contacts or joining the Royal Ocean Racing Club crew list it isn't easy (and I wouldn't advocate seeking RORC membership unless genuinely wanting to race offshore: it isn't fair on the club). The alternative is to equip the yacht properly for hard weather and never go right offshore out of reach of shelter unless you have the nucleus of a strong crew aboard.

Thereafter avoid bad weather when you can and learn from it when you cannot. A racing crew is chosen for its skill and its stamina but a cruising crew is usually friends and family with no special emphasis on either.

A gale is exhilarating for an hour and a wet, frightening, demoralising, noisy and brutish thing thereafter. Strictly speaking a gale is Force 8 on the Beaufort scale (34–40 knots wind), but in truth one man's strong wind is another man's gale. If there is wind and sea enough to make his boat unmanageable and to tax him and his crew beyond their strength – then it is gale enough.

WIND STRENGTH

Study the Beaufort scale in the Appendix. Note the land criteria for Forces 4, 5 and 6, which are the strengths with which we are most familiar. Force 5, fresh breeze 17–21 knots or $19\frac{1}{2}$–$24\frac{1}{2}$ m.p.h., is the sort of wind a cyclist freewheeling down a hill might feel, and gale Force 8, 33–40 knots or 38–46 m.p.h. is roughly double that. If you can find a quiet road on a calm day and get someone to drive your car while you stick your head out of the window at 40 mph you will find that it is hard to keep your eyes wide open and that your ears are filled with the bellow of wind. Yet it is Force 5 which raises all manner of trouble at sea in small yachts: wave trouble, motion trouble, deeply reefed and staggering in just half the strength of a gale.

It is the modern auxiliary engine, more powerful than in older yachts, that gets most of us out of our Force 5 troubles. With only a scrap of sail set we can motor-sail to windward or plug steadily, albeit wetly, upwind with sail stowed. It is a facility to use but not one upon which to base the whole strategy of cruising. In a sailing vessel the ability to perform under sail is the first consideration and the powerful auxiliary is a bonus.

Judging wind strength is not easy. Force 5–6 on a sparkling sunny day and on a reach is sheer bliss. On a dull rainy day or at night it feels frightening. A cold, early season wind has a greater heeling effect than a warm wind of the same m.p.h.; a steady wind of given strength is easier to deal with than a squally wind of the same *average* strength.

The best way to learn to judge wind strength is to invest in a reliable anemometer and make a habit of guessing or judging first and then confirming it. Under way, judging the true wind is harder still since the apparent wind may be greater or less than the true wind, depending on whether you're sailing into or off the wind. The shape and behaviour of the waves will not change – only the factors of fetch, depth and tidal current will do that.

Wind usually rises through a series of hard squalls, each a little more powerful than the one before. For this reason when debating whether to get under way and leave shelter it is sensible to spend at least ten minutes just sniffing, feeling and assessing the wind. What a boat will stand to leeward on the run is one thing but the true test is what she will take when on the wind, and to reiterate what I said earlier, no boat is fully under control, under a particular sail area, unless she can be handled to windward in an emergency. That she could be so handled under engine is only half the answer; engines can fail. In the average 24–30 ft cruiser performance on the run in a steadily rising wind and sea might go something like this.

Running Force 4 Easy to steer, apparent wind scarcely felt, little risk from an accidental gybe, headsail either set wing-and-wing on the opposite side to the mainsail or allowed to fill now and again. Sea slight.

Running Force 5 Helmsman now needs to concentrate. Boat sailing fast and beginning to roll. Headsail fills and collapses with an audible bang. Rising sea astern begins to make steering more difficult but no feeling yet of being over-pressed.

Running Force 6 If the mainsail is still not reefed the steering begins to be wild, tending to broach and a strong roll has developed. Headsail slamming with a vigour that shakes the whole mast. Wave-planing at intervals and sea astern beginning to roll.

Running Force 7 If not reefed by now she will have broached out of control – more frightening than dangerous, but a warning. If well reefed she will be moving at well over her designed speed in a series of wild surges, stern squatting deeply and rolling excessively at times. Headsail slamming with a force that seems likely to take the stick out of her. Sea breaking astern could roll her on her beam ends if she broached at the wrong moment. There is a very real danger of somebody being flung overboard in such a broach. She must be slowed right down, sailed under small headsail only and with the wind a little on one quarter to keep it quiet.

Beating Force 4 Mainsail and genoa. Heeling to perhaps 20° and sailing hard on the wind at her best. Occasional burst of spray and in heavier puffs tending to gripe up or be a little over-pressed.

Beating Force 5 Working jib and two rolls or equivalent slab reef in main, heeling more and butting hard into the head sea with a good deal of flung spray. Still completely manageable but griping up hard in the puffs. An efficient windward-going design will be making good time although wet and uncomfortable. A tubby, high freeboard design begins to wallow, her windage laying her hard over, sails losing drive and windage: sail power ratio becoming unequal. Leeway increases. Time to reef well down and give her a little engine.

Beating Force 6 Deeply reefed main and smallest jib. Good progress in sheltered waters although laid hard over in puffs. In open sea conditions an efficient windward boat is still making fast but very uncomfortable progress in a series of shattering crashes and deluges of water. Less efficient designs now make virtually no headway to windward under sail alone although making progress off the wind. Motor-sailing now only possible under reefed main or the propeller will be out of water for much of the time due to heeling.

Beating Force 7 Deepest reef and storm jib. Efficient design still making to windward but the motion too wild now for careful chartwork or food preparation. Everything below wet and soggy. Less efficient design can only square-drift, making excessive leeway.

The foregoing are generalizations; you have to find out what you, your boat and your crew are capable of coping with. In terms of strategy, though, there is a gradual reduction of choice of direction. In ideal conditions we can lay a course in any direction we choose, from a dead run to a beat. As conditions deteriorate we are eventually left with no choice but a reach or a run and piloting the boat safely through the seas becomes more important than making a passage. If the wind should rise to storm conditions the height, length and behaviour of the seas will be the only factor you can consider – other than sea-room.

If shelter cannot be reached quickly and safely in a gale it should not be attempted. Sweeping statements, though, are very dangerous; every case must be considered separately. There is a great deal of difference between running hell for leather towards a rock-bound lee shore in the hope of finding a river and shelter, and running or reaching off on a course which converges with the coast and a prominent headland behind which there is quieter water and a sheltered approach to that river.

It is not just a matter of wind. The onset of bad weather also means a rapid deterioration of visibility. There is also the matter of shallower water and the very dangerously breaking water there. Also the danger of fast tidal currents running against the wind and, once, again, a dangerously breaking sea. The river which might offer safe entry on the flood could be a death-trap on the ebb and so it is not just a matter of finding the entrance through the driving murk, but of arriving at a suitable time for safe entry.

These are the kind of considerations a skipper has to take into account when deciding whether or not to make for shelter. He may often be far safer to stay at sea. A typical summer gale may not last at full strength for more than 8–12 hours before either moderating or shifting direction – though again one cannot rely on the typical. Singlemindedness is essential. There will be a tendency to seek shelter at all costs which must be resisted. It could well be that the crew must be resigned to blowing to leeward a hundred miles from where they want to be. All that must matter is the safe management of the vessel. If she has sea-room to leeward there is less to worry about. Lying a-hull, a yacht may make a steady 2–3 knots downwind and if she was only 30 miles offshore in the beginning, she will be getting dangerously close to a lee shore after 10–12 hours. A skipper must be constantly watching the wind strength and direction. A sudden shift passing unnoticed could give her a reach to safety or as easily turn a hitherto unmenacing coast into a lee shore. There is one stable fact: any wind shift when a wind has been dead onshore becomes a freeing shift provided a skipper is alert enough to spot it and take advantage of it.

Remaining alert isn't easy. The unbelievable noise, the wild motion and the constant gnawing anxiety has a numbing effect on the mind which allied to natural weariness reduces people to a miserable lethargy. Morale becomes very low. With most of the crew lying on their bunks the remaining active members are more heavily taxed than ever. Everything is wet and cold. There is little chance of producing hot food and it is then a short step from weariness to total fatigue. I paint a deliberately unhappy picture because extreme bad weather at sea is like that and people make foolish decisions that are hard for those who were not there to understand.

EXTREME CONDITIONS

We have considered the consequences of a summer gale of short duration and which rises to Force 7–8 with squalls of up to Force 9 possible. It is a thing to avoid, but having been overtaken by fast–moving extreme conditions it is by no means desperately dangerous provided the yacht is handled wisely and kept away from heavily breaking water. The boat is not totally overpowered; she can be kept under some sort of control and it is then all a question of time, of listening to forecasts and not doing anything rash. No consideration of bad weather at sea in small yachts can ignore the infamous and tragic Fastnet Rock Race of 1979 and its implications for all who cruise at sea.

Let us get things straight, though. There had been warnings of approaching bad weather, of gales, for days before the storm. To offshore racing crews gales hold no fears: both the crews and the boats are shaped to cope with bad weather – and we must except these yachts which were shown to be designed to fit a Rule rather than for their real purpose of keeping the sea. In short, no typical family or ordinary cruising yacht would have attempted more than a series of short coastal hops from shelter to shelter. They would most certainly not have pushed out into the open Atlantic with the rugged Cornish coast and Scilly Isles under their lee and a gale almost upon them.

We all know what happened. The sudden deepening of the depression, the rapid development of Storm Force and then later the dramatic wind shift which drove one train of huge waves across the earlier pattern, resulting in huge and precipitous wave fronts and yachts rolled over like toys. Before we begin sifting some of the lessons learned from that historic drama we must consider how we stand in this. Do we henceforward abandon offshore passage-making until we have a crew and a boat fitted to survive a similar situation or do we equip and crew our boats to cope with the typical summer gale and gamble on avoiding the ultimate? When we drive our cars fast with our families' lives in our hands, we do so knowing that there is always an outside chance of some idiot shooting straight out from an intersection. That is the gamble we take. It is far more likely to happen than a Fastnet Storm. We do all we can to avoid such dangers knowing that with luck and if the worst happened we might still survive. The chances of surviving Storm Force at sea are very much higher than those of surviving a road smash at speed.

In the Fastnet Storm it was the precipitous walls of breaking water moving at speed which did all the damage. Such seas overwhelmed craft of all sizes and designs. Skippers of the different craft tried every known technique in heavy weather procedure and no one approach appeared superior to another. Those yachts which kept a skilled helmsman at the tiller fared marginally better than those which did not, whether they ran off under a scrap of sail (or none at all), kept up speed in the hope of running ahead of the seas, ran with warps out, weaved downwind avoiding the crests or hove-to, or lay closehauled keeping a little headway on their vessels. At another time and place in the same weight of wind but with a less precipitous sea any of these techniques could have been successful.

Fig. 44

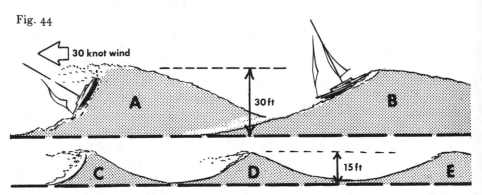

A and B: seas moving at up to 30 knots and averaging some 30 ft high. At A the wave has become unstable and dangerous to a running yacht whereas B, typical of open ocean seas, is not yet dangerous. Waves C, D and E are more typical of the maximum wave types found in English Channel waters in bad conditions. C is an unstable shoaling water wave. E and D are more likely to be met with in deeper water.

Of the yachts which were rolled over, turned upside down or rolled through 360° (some of them several times) one significant fact emerges: *provided the water could be kept out,* the yachts remained afloat with their crews down below. Even those which floated upside down for quite long periods *remained floating.* It seems reasonable then to suppose that given the sea-room to leeward, a watertight hull and deck, and a crew with the courage to batten themselves below, having tried everything else and reached the last pitch of exhaustion, *there is a very good chance of ultimate survival.*

It is easier described than done. The willpower needed to stay below, the confusion, the physical injury resulting from being thrown across the saloon, the bombardment of heavy loose objects and the sheer naked panic of it all cannot be imagined. The Fastnet taught us the importance of being able to secure hatch boards from within, of the need to secure the battery, cooker, toolbox, loose tins of food, and indeed even the bunks. The importance of bilge pumps operable from below, of harness strong points, adequate handholds and emergency lighting (torches) are all stressed.

Perhaps the outstanding lesson was to stay with the boat for as long as she is likely to remain afloat. In many cases abandoning must have occurred because crews *believed* their boats to be in danger of sinking. Even a couple of feet of water inside a hull creates an alarming amount of noise as it surges to and fro, and in the dark it is a determined man who can dismiss the fear of some serious undiscovered leak.

Another unforgettable lesson was that an automatically inflated liferaft offers almost certain salvation from immediate danger in moderate or calm – or even *ordinary* gale – conditions, but in a wind of storm force it is as vulnerable to being torn away, capsized or damaged as any other fabric construction of light weight. It is no reason to condemn liferafts; it merely reinforces the need to stay with the ship until the weather improves or, in real emergency, such as the proximity of a lee shore, injury aboard or similar urgency, the arrival of help in answer to distress signals. Note, however, that there is no guarantee whatsoever that such signals will be seen and answered. In the final count, the crew must behave as though they were responsible for their own salvation.

To summarise: a modern cruiser albeit dismasted and even minus her rudder is unlikely to sink provided her hull and decks remain intact and her hatches can be secured. If she has sea-room her crew have a good chance of survival.

THE SUMMER GALE

The dividing line between danger and the mere discomfort of a summer gale is largely a matter of land, depth of water and tidal current plus of course crew stamina. If it is quite obvious that shelter cannot be reached the skipper must prepare to sail through the weather. He must consider the course he is on. If it is other than dead to windward he will probably be able to continue it, reducing sail to deeply reefed main and storm jib at an early stage and making good any loss of speed by motor-sailing.

This assumes that the course will not become navigationally difficult later on. The last thing he needs is a course beset by navigational hazards when he is fully occupied by handling the boat in worsening weather and when the visibility is down. If this would be the case he must look for easily sailed and navigated alternatives, e.g. out to sea or straight down-Channel perhaps. If this is not feasible either he may well decide that the only safe place to be is more or less where he is; to heave-to or at least sail slowly on any safe course. His aim is to stay away from a dangerous coast, from shoal waters and from areas of fast tide.

Heaving-to under headsail alone or reduced mainsail and storm jib can be surprisingly comfortable – relatively. In a short summer gale it might be for no more than 6–8 hours, or for the hours of darkness; thereafter the yacht may resume if not her original passage, then an acceptable alternative.

Running off is the other choice. It is argued variously that one should either run fast, ahead of the breaking crest, or so slowly that the yacht's wake does not cause the crests to break. In deep open ocean conditions the former seems to have a lot going for it, but in the steeper seas of shallower Continental waters the latter would seem wiser. There is one tricky factor: this constant manning of the helm means that there must be people capable of doing so, which is by no means guaranteed in a family cruiser.

Before the weather worsens the skipper must check up on gear, prepare and if possible eat a good meal, establish his position as accurately as possible, make ready all the gear he is likely to need and of course get his weather forecast up to date by all available means. If he has a radio transmitter aboard he should inform the Coastguard of his position and intentions and if there isn't already a radar reflector hoisted he must rig one.

There is much to be said about bad-weather seamanship, towing warps and so forth. If he has had the foresight to equip his boat with a warp or warps which total 200 yards or so then they too must be laid out ready for streaming astern. In bad weather even the most simple job becomes very difficult.

SPECIAL EQUIPMENT

Under this heading I include items not purely of importance in bad weather but meant for taking the hard work and some of the risk out of passage-making; therefore in conserving effort there is a special advantage when the going becomes taxing.

Roller Headsails Sophisticated versions of the old idea overcome practically all the snags inherent in earlier versions of roller headsails. The uneven rolling which resulted in a badly tensioned leech for instance has been remedied by the solid stay or the luff spar. Modern synthetic sailcloth allows an almost all-purpose weight of cloth to be used and the various winch systems permit the maximum sail area fully unrolled to equal that of a working genoa or larger.

The convenience of such a sail is obvious, but it is the ease of shortening sail without leaving the cockpit, thereby cutting out the risk of a tired man crawling forward, at night, in a squall, that recommends it as an important safety factor. No single roller sail is ever as efficient as a range of three separate sails, each of different cut and weight. On the other hand changing these for every fluctuation in wind strength is exhausting for a small crew and the yacht is by turns under and over canvased. With a roller headsail she is always under the ideal headsail area.

Ideally, the sheet lead is also changed for every alteration of sail area; in practice one can get by with two sheet lead positions. What a roller headsail cannot do is take the place of a proper storm jib. It can be rolled down to a small enough area, but the sail by then is high up the stay and the sheet is so long that it both adds greatly to heeling and proves very hard to sheet flat. With a roller headsail there must also be some provision for setting a storm jib, without having to take down the furled headsail.

In terms of size and cloth weight a storm jib deserving of the name can hardly be too small or too heavy if conditions reach anything like storm force. The weight of the cloth is not only necessary for strength but a heavy sail flogs less destructively. How to set it while leaving the roller headsail up but fully rolled is an individual problem. It is not possible to remove some roller gears and in any case not desirable to try to do battle on the foredeck with large areas of wet sailcloth. If a second stay parallel to the rolled sail cannot be contrived (it cannot be a fixture because it will interfere with the rolling) then an inner forestay or babystay should be rigged. By means of a bottlescrew on a slip it can be set up to a reinforced eye in the deck when needed (Fig. 45).

Fig. 45

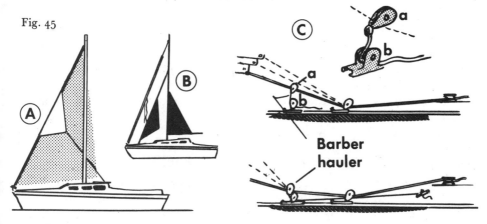

A roller headsail (A) reduced to storm jib size is far too high up the stay. The 'babystay' (B) which can be set up in bad weather and stowed down the shrouds when not needed is an ideal answer to the need for a stay for the storm jib provided its anchorage is good. A Barber hauler (C) can be used to swig down the sheet of a roller headsail thereby altering its lead without the need for crew to leave the cockpit. Block *a* can be a snatch-block and *b* a typical fairlead block.

When choosing roller headsail gear it is important to differentiate between a furling gear and a reefing one. Furling jibs have been around since the early part of this century, small-boat gears with a rotating wooden spar and bigger types having a rotating wire stay. The high degree of torque imposed by a half-rolled sail on a wire stay caused it to partially unwind towards the head, making true reefing impractical. Today's breed are closer to the old wooden roller spars in that they are intended to resist torque.

Furling-only gears are simpler and cheaper; there may even be claims made for them that they double as reefing gears, but it is all a matter of engineering the resistance to torque and the design of roller drum and bearings plus choice of materials to withstand salt and corrosion. Of the two types of roller, one is fully load-bearing in that it replaces the forestay and the other is a roller sleeve turning on a more or less conventional wire forestay – in the latter type it is better to have a dead length forestay which is tightened by adjusting the backstay, but both types are quite satisfactory.

Some more expensive makes of reefing gear permit existing sails to be modified and this means that sails can be changed to suit conditions – a big genoa rolling down to working jib size or perhaps a working jib rolling down to spitfire area. It must be remembered, though, that in neither case will the rolled sail set *quite* as well as a conventional sail of the same area. The alternative of specially cut roller sails has a lot to recommend it. Such a sail can also have a leech panel of ultra-violet ray resistant material to protect against sun-rot when the sail is left rolled on its stay.

Points reefing   Jibs with reef points used to be common, and they are still made either as new sails or by altering existing ones. They have several advantages: no additional equipment to buy or maintain, no need to provide an additional stay for the storm jib as required when there is a foil round the headstay, and a perfect shape can be achieved when the sail is used reefed or unreefed. Although putting in a reef is slower, the procedure is simple and becomes easier with a little practice; also, as the sail remains hanked on it is more tractable when lowered, and less likely to get stuck on the stay partway up or down.

Slab reefing   This idea has been mentioned earlier but I include it here because it guarantees a clean reef in the mainsail and requires only four simple stages to operate: lower, hook on, haul out and hoist again. In many cases this can be cut to two operations since the lowering and hoisting can be carried out from the cockpit. I would not damn roller booms; some are excellent but many are cumbersome and inefficient.

Vane steering   With vane steering I would include self-steering of any kind. For longer passages, though, the wind-vane steering is no drain on electrical power and it is silent. An owner has a bewildering choice of both vane and electrical steering systems and he must take advice. All we can do here is to stress the importance of robustness and to advise against buying the cheapest. These may work quite adequately but are often tedious to set up and adjust. The advantages are obvious: a watch must be kept just the same but the watchkeeper is given freedom of movement and relief from what can in bad or wet weather be a miserable and exhausting chore.

Spray hoods   These and cockpit dodgers create a good deal of windage but both are great conservers of comfort and therefore stamina. For spray hoods there is one vital consideration. Unless it is strong enough when erected to allow crew to hang onto it as they move past there must either be enough width of side-deck for safe passage from one handhold to the next or the lifelines at that point should be reinforced in some way. A person must have his harness hooked up in any case, but when he is frightened to rest his weight on the frail frame of the hood he is halfway to being caught off balance.

Winches – double ratchet and self-tailing   The double ratchet (Gibb) winch simply overcomes the physical problem of getting the handle over the 'hard spot'. A conventional winch with two speeds changed by reversing the rotation leaves the operator with a test of strength to complete a revolution of the handle through the position where the handle is farthest away and gives least leverage. The double ratchet obviates this unfair strain. When a winch crew may be a lightweight and when the boat is heeling this aspect of crewing can become a problem only resolved by increasing winch size at great expense. Self-tailing winches come into this same strength-saving category by permitting two-handed winding, or tandem use if two people are available to use one hand each from opposing sides.

Radio tape recorder   While at sea on passage it is very desirable to catch every shipping forecast thereby building up a continuous picture of the prevailing weather pattern; usually it is part of the watch duties to take down any forecast. Periods in harbour are apt to mean gaps in the weather picture. An automatically time-set recorder makes it possible to tape every forecast in full, some manually when crew are awake and others by timer. While by no means an essential, such a radio is invaluable especially during unsettled periods.

Aft-leading halyards   Some cruisers lend themselves to having halyards led aft to the cockpit while others result in a messy arrangement which only complicates operations. When it is possible to do so easily and neatly the facility of being able to hoist and lower from the cockpit halves the work for the man forward.

Safe sea berths   Surprisingly few offshore cruising yachts can sport more than two secure and comfortable berths in which the crew can rest properly in bad weather. Saloon settees can have side screens of really heavy fabric which can be set up very taut. These will not then allow a sleeper to bulge halfway across the saloon. Proper rest below is vitally important. To *feel* secure, contained, has a great effect upon morale.

Cabin heaters   Permanent, properly vented heaters which can safely be used in hard wet weather are also morale-boosting. They also dry out the air below and contribute to general health. They can be of any type provided they do not smell, upsetting queasy stomachs. Blower types have a secondary role; the steady purring of the fan is a great sleep-inducer.

EXERCISE 1   Emergencies in bad weather

The simplified chart (Fig. 46) shows the mid-English Channel area with shelter ports (S) reachable day or night depending on visibility and other conditions. The wavy lines denote areas of dangerous tidal overfalls and races to be avoided.

You are skippering a sound and well-found modern 30 ft auxiliary sailing cruiser. She has no ship/shore radio but all the usual navigational aids and safety equipment. Your crew includes two fit but not very experienced adults and an experienced man of almost 70 who cannot be looked to for sustained physical effort. The tide, at springs, is just beginning to run to the west and it is June. The latest shipping forecast speaks of a small but rapidly deepening low moving NE from SW of Ireland, passing north of your area, winds gale force 8 imminent.

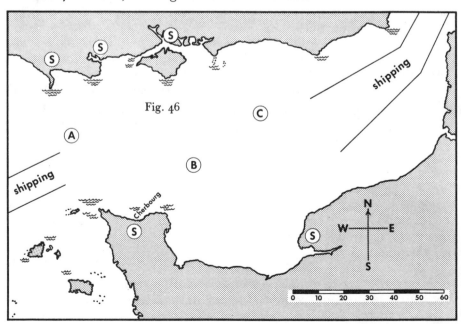

Fig. 46

Make your plan, starting from position A and assuming that you are on a southerly course. Consider your probable position at the various times shown in the table and refer to the code letters for further information about the mishaps and situations which occur and which will alter your plans. Having worked through from position A, repeat the exercise from positions B and C.

POSITION A	POSITION B	POSITION C
1800 A–D–C	1800 D–H	1800 H–J–B
2200	2200 F–E	2200
0100 I–J	0100	0100 F–M
0400	0400	0400
0600	0600	0600 K–G
1000 N–M	1000 G–L	1000
1200	1200	1200
1600	1600	1600
1800	1800	1800

A   Port shroud plates creaking badly and a leak there.
B   Hit floating wreckage. Rudder feels sloppy but no visible damage.
C   You see a distress rocket to windward.
D   All except you and the old man helplessly seasick below.
E   Jib halyard parts and flies aloft.
F   Navigation lights fail.
G   Wind now NW Force 8–9.
H   Wind now W Force 8.
I   Wind now SE Force 7–8.
J   Visibility down to 100 yards with rain also.
K   Crew falls against compass, breaking it.
L   Mystery leak develops. Needs pumping every 10 minutes or the cabin sole is awash (shallow bilges).
M   You sprain your right wrist badly.
N   Log out of action.

When you have completed the three exercises read the following notes.

From Position A
Despite being shorthanded, the law of the sea and common humanity demand that you investigate the distress rocket. By now deeply reefed you might get upwind still, perhaps engine assisted. We must assume that nothing is found and you resume your course. Did you decide to go back to the English coast or did you head off for Cherbourg? Did you continue on your original course, perhaps for the Channel Islands? The islands might be difficult to find in the bad visibility to be expected, and they would make a dangerous lee shore. Cherbourg is over 40 miles away plus tide, but it would be tempting to carry on. The big bay to the

east might offer shelter if you couldn't easily make Cherbourg. Returning to England also means putting a heavier strain on that port shroud, although you could motor with a small jib set.

0100. Whichever course you chose the wind, now in the SE with very bad visibility, is right on the nose if you headed for Cherbourg and you'd be among shipping too. If you had headed back to England you would either have managed to make shelter in time or you would now be off a dangerous lee shore and it would be too risky in that visibility to chance closing the land. Navigation in wild conditions would now be very inaccurate.

1000. The loss of the log is less serious than the sprained wrist, since you cannot do much with it and the old man could not be sent forward to handle sails. By now you are presumably back in mid-Channel. The others below must be made to share the hardship. Perhaps heave-to and wait.

From Position B

With the wind westerly and a west-going tide you should be able to reach Cherbourg deeply reefed or perhaps under jib and engine.

2200. Well, the jib didn't help for long and the loss of the navigation lights in an area which may be used by shipping is no comfort. We hope that a good radar reflector has been hoisted. The nav lights would not have been easy to see in any case.

1000. In the elapsed 12 hours you would probably have made harbour, or perhaps you headed for that bay to find shelter from the westerly gale. With the wind now veering to the NW and blowing harder it seems likely that the gale is almost over (watch the barometer). Meanwhile, if you were in that bay you are now on a lee shore. The only escape would now lie to the east.

From Position C

A Force 8 westerly gale, a suspect rudder and visibility down to 100 yards. Plainly a course for shelter behind the island or an adjoining port. The alternatives of heaving-to or running down-Channel might impose even greater strains on the rudder although heaving-to might be quite possible if the rudder jams or fails while en route. If you can make 6 knots you should be in shelter before 0100 when the navigation lights fail and you sprain your wrist, provided the visibility has improved a little: otherwise it would call for some very careful navigation and in the worst of conditions. If you are still at sea by then you will not be feeling your best and brightest.

0600. No compass now and the wind has veered NW F 8–9. To be still at sea suggests that you did heave-to. According to which tack you used you would by now be either close to the English coast or back in mid-Channel. About all you could do would be to stay hove-to in the expectation that a moderation was not far off.

EXERCISE 2   Wind strength

It is very important to be able to judge wind strength with fair accuracy. Use a hand anemometer to check your own estimates of true wind strength. Note the state of sea and relate it to tidal conditions, shelter etc. Sail downwind and measure apparent wind force, then put the boat on the wind and check it again.

EXERCISE 3   Sail carrying

What do you know about your boat in her ability to carry sail in a steadily increasing wind? Consider and fill in the following table.

If you have never tried reefing to the maximum possible, experiment afloat, considering sheeting angles, sail balance and ease of operation. Are the sheet winches sufficiently powerful? Will they flatten a storm jib in a gale Force 8? Also consider headsail changing in a sudden wind increase to F 8. Can the forehatch be used, would netting or zig-zag cord between the lifeline wires help to control a loose sail?

FORCE	SAIL CARRIED	PERFORMANCE TO WINDWARD	
		sheltered water	*open sea*
4–5	— —
5–6	— —
6–7	— —
Gale	— —

EXERCISE 4   Becoming weather-conscious

Establish daily habits. If possible listen to at least one shipping forecast and/or television forecast giving synoptic chart and outlook. Study the weather map in your daily paper. Try to build up a non-stop situation picture of the existing and forecast weather pattern.

Each morning and evening:

(*a*) Look at the sky. Note cloud type and movement, colour etc and see how it fits the forecast situation.

(*b*) Note wind direction and force, whether steady, gusty etc also whether it feels moist or dry/cold. Estimate its force.

(*c*) Look at your barometer and note the tendency. Each morning, having made an appraisal of the weather and its likely trend for the next 12 hours or so, ask yourself 'Would I now feel happy about making an open-sea passage?' Each evening check whether your decision would have been a wise one.

EXERCISE 5   Seeking shelter

Take any chart and study a coastline. Imagine yourself to be 12 miles offshore and with an onshore gale forecast as imminent. What shelter havens are there? What would the tidal situation be on arrival? Would it be better to beat further offshore while there is still time? Carry out this exercise whenever you have a chart in front of you and a few minutes to spare.

CHAPTER XI

Big Ship versus Small Yacht

Situations

1 You are at sea in daylight and there has been a big container ship which has been on a converging course for the past ten minutes. There is nothing else about and you are not in a Separation Zone; you rely upon your entitlement as a sailing vessel and stand on. As the distance closes you decide to play safe and alter course to pass close astern. She also alters towards you; you alter course back to your original heading *just as she also alters back to hers.* You are now very close . . . what would you do?

2 It is a black night and you are reaching at 4 knots. A big ship to windward of you is due to pass ahead at a distance of perhaps 3 miles and she is no danger. To leeward there are two other ships crossing, but due to pass safely astern of you. The first ship is about 4–5 miles off the coast. Suddenly she alters towards you, seemingly to pass astern and to windward of you. When she is ¼ mile to windward of you she suddenly alters course 90° and comes full at you (Fig. 47). What happened? What can you do?

3 You are closehauled and on a converging course with a ship. You bear off a fraction to pass round her stern but not wishing to lose ground downwind and downtide you do so gradually – just enough to shave round her stern. Nevertheless although *you* can see that you have borne off enough, your bows are still pointing as if to pass ahead of the ship. When you are both very close she suddenly blows one blast and turns hard a'starboard, full at you. Why, and what do you do?

4 You are crossing a busy estuary at night. A big ship is coming up to your port side and you watch her until her masthead and navigation lights show that you are safely across her and some half mile ahead of her. You relax. Suddenly she is once more heading full at you, masthead lights in line, and now very close. What might have caused her change of course and what can you do?

It is perhaps better to deal with the above Situations right at the start of the chapter. All of them happened to me at some time or other and all taught me a lot. In Situation 1 we have a classic case of uncertainty.

This entitlement of sail having right of way over power on the high seas is a dangerous thing to take for granted. Big ships usually do alter for us, but now and again they do not. In this particular case I would imagine that the officer of the watch was not told of my presence until quite late. We both altered together. It was like the little dance people do when meeting nose-to-nose on a stairway, but infinitely more dangerous. On the occasion I turned 180° put my engine on and got the hell out of it because I knew that I could turn faster than she could.

In Situation 2, I was run down. I was skippering a 50 ton gaff schooner and there was no time to start my engine – it meant leaving the deck and going below. We were not sunk, but we were badly mauled by a glancing blow from 13,000 tons of ship. What happened was that a junior watch officer panicked. He found himself on a collision course with the two inward-bound vessels to leeward of me and he dare not alter course towards the land. Having shaped to pass ¼ mile to windward of me he found that he was still on a collision course with one of the other ships, and accordingly he altered dramatically and without considering the small

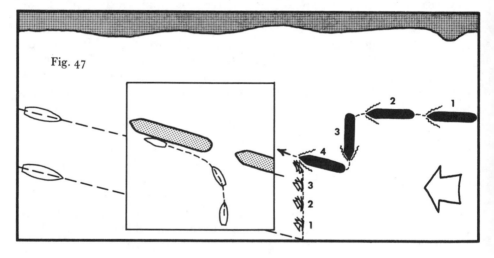

Fig. 47

vessel in the middle of the group. On that occasion I had no choice of manoeuvre. The ship was weaving from side to side following her heavy turn and it was impossible to know which side of us she'd pass or whether she'd hit us, and at her 15–20 knots there was very little time to do anything. Sheer fear made me do the right thing. I rammed the wheel hard down, the fastest direction of turn in that ship on a reach and an instinctive running away reaction. She came down on us in three great bounds and fell alongside just as we came off before the wind. I had instinctively presented her with the *smallest target possible*.

Situation 3 was my fault. I made only a small alteration of course. *I could see that it was enough, but the ship's helmsman could not.* If you alter it should be done boldly, demonstrably, and thereafter the heading should be held. Small alterations or twitching around from course to course are confusing. Luckily I understood his sound signal of one blast (turning to starboard) and I tacked at once. She passed within feet and I was treated to the wigging from the bridge that I deserved.

Situation 4 is one which catches yachtsmen out again and again. A dredged channel in which big ships have a right of way due to their need to stay in the deeper water and a small yacht which can sail where she wishes, in terms of depth. I had forgotten that the channel had a slight bend in it at that point. The ship reached a particular buoy just after I had (as I thought) passed safely ahead of her and then she altered course again, which brought her back on a collision heading. I knew that she was constrained by her depth and that she would not be able to alter course for me. I did as on another occasion, altered right round 180° and got the hell out.

Although it would be quite wrong to foster a feeling of antagonism between yacht and big-ship seaman the fact is that there is a sort of David and Goliath attitude on the part of yachtsmen. The yachtsman is a pain in the neck to a great many big-ship men and unhappily they are often justified in this attitude. Likewise the careful yachtsman, despite his efforts to comply with the Rules finds again and again that big ship behaviour is woefully at fault and frighteningly unpredictable.

We must always remember that this is not a ship-to-ship relationship but a person-to-person one. People control ships and people can be careless and careful; forebearing, impatient; pleasant and unpleasant. They can also have hangovers and belly aches.

It is a two part problem; being seen and *knowing* that you have been seen. We must obey the Rules with understanding. It is not a bit of good being legally blameless when 50,000 tons of legal wrongness is barrelling down on you. So we must do all we can to observe Rules and correct procedures while holding ourselves ready to take any action necessary to avoid collision. In a collision we can only lose.

We have to watch the other ship and try to understand what she may do, or if she is behaving in a particular manner why she is doing so. A ship may appear to be altering for us while in fact she is altering on to a new route heading, or to take early avoiding action concerning another big ship still many miles away. No ship is safely past until it is impossible for her to hit us without turning more than 90° (as I found to my cost). It may often seem impossible for the big ship not to have seen the yacht, but there are many cases of collision or near collision in broad daylight that refute this. Recently, sailing home from the Azores, I met up with a ship way out in the Atlantic. There was nothing else in sight. I watched her from being a distant speck on a sunlit horizon until she was in a close collision situation. She never wavered from her course: I had to throw the yacht about in frantic haste. I had not been seen.

It pays to read about commercial shipping, tankers, ferries, fishermen and their problems and their requirements. Big ships are not always easy to steer, neither is the man at the wheel always very expert or attentive. Small coasters need very special watching. A quartermaster may over-correct on a turn and get a swing on the ship which results in a series of swings before she is steady, or she may be in ballast and having trouble with a beam wind. Big ships cannot stop very easily either. Nobody in his right senses steps out on to a pedestrian crossing in front of a big truck on a wet road. It may take several miles for a big tanker or bulk carrier to make a crash stop and she may do costly damage to her machinery in the process.

Radar solves far fewer problems than yachtsmen realize. A modern radar, expertly used and tuned for it, can pick up an oil drum in the water far ahead of the ship. Often it is not expertly used and is tuned to a range band far beyond the small yacht ahead only a mile away. Neither can one rely upon the watch lookout. He may be alert and in constant com-munication with the bridge by phone, or the lookout may be the officer of the watch who just happens to be working on the chart. If the helmsman doesn't see you the ship may run you down.

Big ships must make fast or at any rate punctual passages to be profitable. A dock berth has been booked, a lock gate has to be caught on a particular tide and so on. They cannot afford to slow down or weave around every yacht in their way and they don't. Many are bullies. If they stand on, the yacht will alter. Hundreds of conscientious ship's officers alter for yachtsmen and render assistance at enormous cost. Likewise there are hundreds of yachtsmen who repeatedly cross close ahead of big ships without a thought.

I remember speaking to a ship's officer about sightings of yachts at sea. 'When I was a cadet on my first watch,' he said, 'I reported everything I saw or thought I saw, mostly false alarms. The mate gave me a real bawling out. After that I kept my mouth shut until I was absolutely certain.' The frightening thing about that conversation was that many hundreds of small yachts ply the sea at night with lights so poor that they are never more than half-seen – and so not reported.

Every yacht that sails by night must carry navigation lights in accordance with International Maritime Law in terms of their position and brilliance. The combination masthead lights now permitted for small sailing craft are far superior to side or pulpit combination lights, which are often half-obscured by heeling or sails. Owners should have both. When under power a yacht must be lit as for a powered vessel, which means a masthead sectored white *above* her red and green sidelights. It is important to avoid anomalous situations at night.

What is less often considered is the range of lights. Navigation lights may begin the night at full power, but by the end of it a single battery, perhaps only half-charged at commencement, may be very low. Some owners have a dangerous policy of sailing without lights when no other lights are in sight. Almost every owner I have spoken to about this can relate a story of a near miss when meeting another yacht doing just this same thing. Ideally a yacht should have two batteries, one for domestic and general use and the other which can be isolated for navigation lights only. Much depends on how much night sailing is done, but it only needs one incident on one night for a serious accident to occur. All yachts should carry a very powerful hand torch in any case. A sailing yacht is a relatively slow moving craft. At 4–5 knots or less she is virtually stopped in the water when compared to a ship making 18–20 knots. The first essential is to be seen.

The best use for a powerful torch is to sight it steadily towards the approaching ship and hold it for perhaps half a minute, then pan it slowly up the sails and back for another long hold. Never flash it – unless you are capable of dealing with the stream of Morse which may follow. A steady, direct light can be seen from a far greater distance than the diffused glow of reflected light from a sail.

The minimum range requirement for a small yacht's red and green is one mile. Red has a much lower range than white, and green is lower still. It is very easy for a ship to get to within half a mile of a yacht with a weak battery or on a night of poor visibility. In a crossing situation it is wiser to assume that we have not been seen, while behaving in full accordance with the law. A change of course to pass astern of the ship, made well in advance of need, is the only safe answer. It is when there is a second and perhaps a third big ship following the first at intervals of perhaps a couple of miles that a yacht needs to make absolutely sure that she has been seen in plenty of time by those following. It is illegal to switch on spreader lights and other non-navigation lights, but *in certain circumstances* it is seamanlike provided it does not lead to confusion. Ask any watch officer from a big ship and he will tell you that he doesn't give a damn what you switch on so long as he can see you and assess the direction in which you're sailing and your intentions.

When all else fails, when you have done all you can to attract attention and the ship has still turned towards you, there is the white flare. This pyrotechnic must be kept in a clip, in a dry place but within reach of the hand from the cockpit. The searing white light has terrific power and no big ship man can fail to see it and take avoiding action, provided you have left him time to do so. If a white flare is used you must avoid looking at it or anywhere near it or your night vision will be destroyed in the blackness which will follow when it goes out.

TRAFFIC SEPARATION SCHEMES

There have always been areas in which big ships have right of way by reason of being constrained by their draft. Port approaches, harbours, rivers, estuaries and so on are covered by local byelaws and yachts may not hinder big ships. More lately have come the Traffic Separation Schemes at such key areas as the Dover Straits, off the Dutch/Belgian coast and Ushant, etc. Ships are routed to separate oncoming traffic and there is a no-man's land or Separation Zone to divide them. These Separation Zones are keenly policed by the authorities of neighbouring countries by sophisticated and very powerful radar as well as patrol boats and spotter aircraft. Ships passing through and seeing a transgressor will also report. To date there have been a number of heavy fines imposed, and a great many cases brought to court and acquitted with a warning. Yachtsmen, sadly, have been prime offenders; they also have difficulties to contend with that are not experienced by bigger vessels.

The Coastguard is quite specific. Yachts lacking speed (indeed all yachts) should where possible avoid Separation Schemes altogether. If they cannot avoid them they should cross each stream of traffic at right angles to the approaching vessels or at an angle *with* the flow. Never under any circumstances *against* the traffic flow.

Sometimes this is easier said than done. A strong tidal current may mean that although the yacht is crossing ahead of a ship properly on a heading at right angles to her course, the yacht's *course over the ground* and therefore her image on the shore radar display may show her to be proceeding aslant and *against* the flow of traffic. This point has been made to the authorities. While no rewording of the Rules has taken place to allow for this situation, HM Coastguard has stated that 'the circumstances of wind and current will always be assessed and allowed for by an experienced officer on duty, should such a case of apparent rule-breaking be reported.' With this we have to be content.

Headwinds blowing across a lane constitute another problem for the auxiliary sailing yacht. With a choice of tacks a skipper must choose that which sets him across and *with* the flow of traffic (A). With a strong tide to consider, he may try to lee-bow the current and thus make a right angle crossing over the ground (B) (Fig. 48).

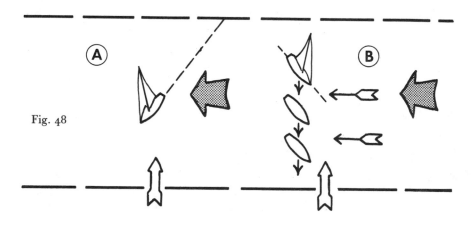

Fig. 48

In effect, though, his bows will not then be at right angles to approaching traffic. The only real solution in such a case is to motor square across albeit head to wind. With a low power auxiliary engine, a fresh or strong wind and a head sea this may result in a laboured and very slow passage; thus it is no solution at all, for the longer the yacht remains in the busy lane the longer she is at risk, especially by night. In such a case a skipper can do only one thing; sail closehauled on the down-lane tack even though it is also down-tide and may lose him precious ground when he resumes his course later.

Having negotiated one lane, and the Separation Zone, the other lane must then be dealt with and this time (in this case) the skipper may lawfully lee-bow the tide if he chooses (Fig. 49).

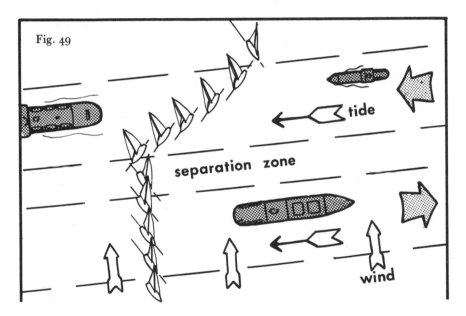

Fig. 49

A separation area is well buoyed and perhaps there will be light vessels stationed at either end. We are advised, when practicable, to detour around the ends of such areas but in fact it is often more dangerous to become mixed up with a mass of big ships which are sorting themselves out prior to, or following, navigation through the area.

What is of more importance is to know when we reach the area. Unless we navigate to pick up one of the flanking buoys it is quite possible to blunder into a lane without realising it. I broke the law quite unintentionally off the Lizard, having made my landfall from the open Atlantic. I was expecting the Separation Zones and seeing a big ship proceeding west assumed that she was in her proper lane, shaping my own course accordingly. Only later, when beset by four ships sailing contrary to my own heading, did I realise that the first ship had been a 'rogue'. Had I identified a flanking buoy first of all I would not have made what might have been a costly mistake.

Judging the speed of oncoming ships is not easy. It is also much affected by visibility and by the size and type of ship involved. In a haze a coaster looks much larger on first sighting than she is. Ships when sighted in the distance appear to be moving very slowly. As the gap narrows they seem to put on speed until they suddenly grow and close the gap at an alarming rate. The bow wave is some help as an indication of speed, but a light-laden bulbous-bowed ship travelling quite slowly pushes up what appears to be a huge bow wave. The only sure procedure is to watch the angle of convergence.

By holding a straight course and by holding your head quite still you can sight on a distant ship by lining her up with some part of your rail. If after several minutes she is still seen poised over a stanchion, if she has not shifted forward of it, she is likely to be on a potential collision course. The accepted check is to take careful compass bearings of her at five minute intervals from first sighting, then more frequently as she closes. So long as the two courses, ship and yacht, are at a wide enough angle, around 90°, the method is reliable and continues to be reliable right up to the time for taking action, if needed. A narrow angle, though, can be very unreliable and becomes even less reliable as the distances narrow. Add to this the difficulty of taking accurate bearings in a moving yacht and it is highly suspect (Fig. 50).

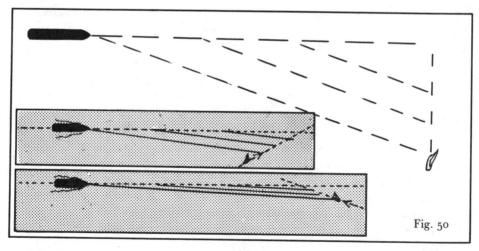

Fig. 50

Big ship men cannot always assess the speed of a yacht very accurately either and I was once almost run down when sailing at night at over 15 knots in a catamaran. The watch officer must have identified us as a sailing yacht from our lights and perhaps not used radar. He made to cross our bows, suddenly put on about 45° of helm to cut round our stern, and then altered back just as I had borne off hard in response to his first alteration. Ships' officers, unless they have done some yachting, know very little about small sailing craft, their speeds or their ability to manoeuvre.

In addition to the very large ships we have to pay special attention to a host of other and specialised craft. At night, if a vessel carrying puzzling lights appears on a converging course or ahead of you the only safe thing to do is slow right down to the point of bare steerage way until you can consult the almanac and find out just what she is and what she may be doing. A tug towing an oil platform on a wet and windy night for instance, or any sort of tow, is highly dangerous if the tow is a long one and inviting a passage between. Fishing craft are also puzzling. Either avoid them by a very wide berth or stop and find out what they are doing. A trawler with gear down, a drifter, a couple of pair trawlers or seine netters, all behave very differently, carry different lights and on occasion behave with complete disregard for the Rules. Fishermen are earning their living. They exhibit lights to protect them from other vessels and thereafter take little or no notice of nearby vessels. When a crabber is shooting pots one false move can mean a very nasty death for the man whose job it is to heave the linked pots overboard as the boat plunges ahead.

YACHTS AND RADAR

All yachts at sea should carry a radar reflector permanently aloft. By doing so they have gone some way towards appearing on the display of a ship's radar set as a consistent echo to be identified as another vessel. It is absolutely no guarantee that they are therefore safe, for the reasons already discussed and because a radar reflector may not be doing its job.

The basic octahedral reflector of 18 in. corner to corner gives a good consistent echo *when it is displayed at the ideal height and angle*. When a yacht is heeled at approaching 30° the ability to reflect decreases rapidly. If its angles are other than exactly 90° between faces, again it loses efficiency. If it is masked by wet sails and less than 10 ft from sea level it might just as well be left below.

There are now other designs available which offer a wider arc of return signal and therefore continue to be efficient in a heeling yacht, but it is important to see reports of tests on such reflectors before buying them because there are a number of quite ingenious reflectors on the market which, apart from folding up with magical simplicity, are virtually useless.

In rough weather the problem for the radar set user is wave clutter, rain belts, the interference of other nearby sets in use, and the fact that the radar watch may be scanning far ahead on range bands which exclude or obscure small echoes a couple of miles away. If an opportunity ever arises to visit a ship's bridge and talk to a deck officer on the subject of yachts and radar it should be taken. It is not always very reassuring.

The ideal place for a radar reflector in a sailing yacht is right on top of the mast. It is also usually quite out of the question for a number of reasons – wind instruments, a tri-colour navigation light and windage are some of them. Suspended from a crosstree is a poor alternative because the reflector is often masked by wet nylon or Dacron/Terylene, which is a barrier to radar pulses, and so only the backstay remains. Here it can foul the sail, also it imposes a weight on the stay which causes it to jerk about. It is up to an owner to puzzle around this problem according to his own particular problem. The final alternative, and a good one, is a jointed pole which mounts right forward from the pulpit and raises the reflector to a height of maybe 10–12 ft from the sea. This is still too low for the best results in terms of range and it is not really high enough above the waves. A big ship's radar scanner may be 80 ft or more above the sea, from which angle the almost sea level reflector in a small yacht is virtually among the waves. The reflection it gives must be very good and very consistent if it is to be singled out for attention.

Consistency of signal is vital. An oil drum now and then returns a strong signal, but a radar target must be presented at right angles to the beam and remain there (octahedral and other designed reflectors 'juggle' with the signal in order to do this). The hull of a yacht and her mast present a flickering signal which could as easily be a wave or flotsam.

The value of a radar reflector lies in knowing its imperfections and allowing for them. Without one we are often quite invisible to a ship's radar operator, with one we have a strong chance of being seen and identified as another vessel.

EXERCISE 1   Know your Collision Rules

Study the International Regulations for Preventing Collisions at Sea in your almanac and then attempt to answer the following questions.

(Answers in the Appendix.)
1. At night, should you be able to see a ship's stern light simultaneously with her side lights? Are her masthead lights visible when her stern light is visible?
2. A ship must be over 20 m in length before she must carry two masthead lights: right or wrong?
3. What range of visibility should the anchor light of a yacht of less than 12 m be?
4. You are closehauled at night on starboard tack and to windward you see the port light of another yacht getting closer: what would you assume?
5. You are on a collision course with a big ship. She blows two blasts on her siren. What will she probably do next?
6. Green light above a white one. What is this vessel doing?

EXERCISE 2 Observation

When sailing, watch the shipping and note the following:

When the bow wave of a ship lifts above the horizon can you also distinguish portholes, her boats, flags?

At night note the relative brightness of white and red/green lights, and the stage at which individual lit-up portholes can be seen.

By day or night, when viewing an approaching ship try to guess how long it will be before she reaches a certain point (a buoy perhaps). This is a very interesting test of judgement.

Note when you can hear an approaching ship. It will vary greatly with wind direction, wave noise, humidity etc.

Try to identify commercial ships. Read up a little on modern shipping and the behaviour of ships, their cargoes and their destinations. It often helps to be able to identify a particular vessel, thereby having some idea of her passage and slowest speeds, and turning, manoeuvring and stopping capabilities.

EXERCISE 3 Crossing angles

Working on a convenient chart which shows a shipping route, plot a typical crossing situation. Yacht and ship on a right-angle crossing course. Ship making 12 knots, yacht making 4. Determine where the yacht would have to be before the situation became dangerous. How many minutes would elapse? (See Fig. 51). Repeat using other angles and speeds.

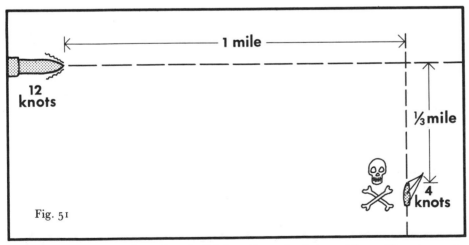

Fig. 51

At sea when crossing ahead of ships, time the interval from the moment when you have a ship's masts in line to the time when she crosses astern of your track. Invite your regular crew to join in with these exercises. There will be times when they will have to make the decision to stand on or call you to take charge.

CHAPTER XII

Emergencies

Situations

Man overboard
Fire
Holing at sea
Fog
Collision

Dragging anchor
Dismasting
Wreck
Rescue by ship or aircraft

There is no need to invent situations to illustrate the emergencies listed, they speak from themselves. Collectively they suggest that the sea is a very dangerous place, but we could as profitably list the emergencies of the home and earmark them for consideration. A motor lawnmower is a lethal machine, a ladder an invitation to disaster.

Since people and the decisions they make are the root cause of most emergencies, any consideration of the remedies must be related to people and how they are likely to behave in a crisis. The best thought out emergency action possible founders at once if the crew cannot carry it out. A yachtsman psychiatrist once told me that in crisis people are likely to react in various ways. Some just freeze up, others fly into vigorous action without any thought at all, yet others begin to shout orders right left and centre, or in a mighty endeavour to remain calm achieve calmness and little else. Hopefully there is one person who keeps his or her head and does the right thing at once. If this happens there is then a good chance that other right things will be done and confidence will return to the rest of the crew who themselves begin to act sensibly. The danger lies in the risk of the loudest mouth seizing control.

This is why drills are evolved. A drill must not be a mindless robot reaction followed through doggedly and irrespective of whatever else may be happening. A drill fills the interval between initial shock when the brain may be temporarily out of gear and the moment when reason can take over. A man-overboard drill might be followed closely, phase by phase, but when somebody is knocked unconscious by the boom during a gybe and a rope fouls the propeller (this once happened), the man overboard drill suddenly needs drastic modification.

Drills, then, must be very simple and uncomplicated. Immediate action would be a better description. Equally important is that all these emergencies and any others should have been mulled over well in advance, discussed and agreed upon. This is a skipper and mate task; there is no point in delivering heavyweight lectures to a family crew, to the terror of nervous members who are first-timing and the round-eyed wonderment of children. Discussed they should be, though and perhaps the best of all ways is to follow the lead of at least one yacht club I know and make up winter evening discussion groups presided over by someone who really knows the score.

MAN OVERBOARD

This is a double problem: the handling of the yacht in bringing her to a standstill alongside the person in the water and the second and often larger problem of hauling him back aboard. I would strongly advise that a volunteer in a lifejacket should act as guinea pig right from the start of any man overboard exercise, allowing himself to be hauled aboard and offering a little but not much assistance. In real life he may be deeply chilled, very frightened, exhausted by panic attempts to struggle up the topsides. He may even be unconscious. One of the most frightening experiences of my life was trying to recover a man from the water. There were two of us trying to get him through the lifeline wires and all three of us reached the point of exhaustion. Of late years the increasing height of topsides in designs has heightened the problem proportionately. Remember also that what may be possible in an offshore racing yacht with a crew of fit young men is dangerously different in a family cruiser when it may be the skipper who goes overboard and the wife and kids who have to cope with getting him back.

Handling the boat   The long-held school solution is to GYBE AT ONCE. The only real benefit of this drill is that it is something to do during that interval when the mind is struggling to cope with shocked disbelief.

On a reach or closehauled, gybing has the virtue of putting the boat downwind of the person in the water, but gybing on a run achieves nothing and invites a frap-up in any case. If one gybes *instantly* from reaching or closehauled the boat comes round in a circle that stops her almost dead in the water on the man to be rescued. The odds are very much against any helmsman being able to react so quickly, and even if he did the rest of the crew would be quite unready to deal with the situation and the boat would have filled and borne off by the time they were ready. Gybing is something to do. It jerks a crew from its state of frozen horror but that passes quickly in any case provided somebody can take effective charge (Fig. 52A).

Current thought on the best method of returning to the man in the water is to put the boat on a REACH the instant he goes over and sail straight, watching him the whole time and gybing for the return reach as soon as the ship is under control. On a reach, the sheets eased and sailing away from the man prior to return, the boat will be quieter, under better control and heeling less. All of which facilitates crew movement and affords a better opportunity to keep watch on the man. On the return, and a little to leeward of him, boat speed can be controlled exactly, slowing to a final stop just to leeward of him (Fig. 52B).

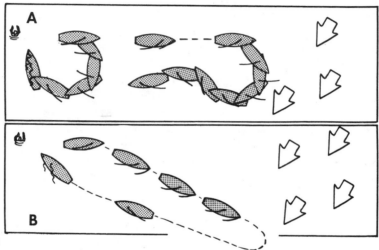

Fig. 52

A. An instant gybe would bring the boat back to the man in the water, but if delayed a gybe would have the sole merit of putting the boat to leeward of him prior to a reach back.
B. The reach off and reach back technique has replaced the old gybe-at-once drill formerly advocated.

To leeward or to windward? This is where the drill begins to break down. If a boat is to leeward of the man and she heels even a little her topside height is greatly increased: he is beyond arm's reach. If she is to windward of him and she heels a little it is decreased – indeed men have been rolled aboard over a lee rail without any effort as the boat heeled down. The danger is that the side pressure of a boat stopped and drifting beam-on tends to pull a man in the water down under the hull. The person in charge has to decide. What *can* happen is that the man is grasped just as the boat, left to her own devices, fills aback and heels hard over breaking the rescuer's hold.

This is where the value of knowing your boat's behaviour comes in. In a small crew where all hands will be needed to get the person aboard it must be possible to leave the boat to look after herself, lying beam-on to wind and sea. If she will do this then it doesn't matter on which side of the man in the water she brings up because he can be towed around to the low lee side.

All this is still too much for one frightened person and maybe a couple of kids left on board to cope with; there must be an even simpler drill.

In my own boat we are a husband and wife team and we have evolved our own drill. Here it is: If I should go O.B. my wife will turn the boat back as fast as she can and sail past me close enough to actually put a lifebuoy into my hands – it doesn't matter how fast she is going, she has *bought time.* Knowing that she has bought time would calm her, give her time to think. She can now either manoeuvre the boat back and slow her alongside in the ordinary manner, or if it is a wild day she has another option. On the stern we have a lifebuoy with a light and a drogue (to prevent it from being wind-drifted out of reach) and also a 60 ft coil of floating line with a floating quoit at its end; the line is attached to the stern but the lifebuoy is free-floating. The two are held secure by twin loops of shockcord joined by a wooden peg which has a bright red tag on it. One tug and away they go.

The idea then is for her to release lifebuoy and line astern. The lifebuoy is there if I need it but the 60 ft line follows in the wake of the yacht and she must sail round me in a curve to drag it into my grasp. Once that is achieved she stops the yacht, letting fly both sheets completely and secures the tiller to leeward. There are two shockcord bights permanently there for that purpose.

The rest of the drill is commonsense. Both lifeline wires and spray dodgers are on a quick release system and can be dropped flat. On each side of the boat is a line permanently rove and weighted which forms a bight that falls down into the water and into which I could put my foot, buying time again. The final detail is to rig out the boarding ladder. It all depends on one thing: that I remain conscious. If it ever happens and I don't remain conscious then it won't help much. The best man overboard remedy is a safety harness worn and used. I am as remiss as the next man: I wear and use it when there seems reason to do so.

The whole question of dragging a heavy person aboard by brute force must be abandoned. You are capable of one major physical effort and so is he; the next attempt is a weaker one and the next weaker still. Fear lends initial added strength but the body having made its total effort can do no more. A proper boarding ladder projecting right down into the water with steps, not rope or broomstick rungs, is essential, but it must be capable of being secured to the rail, not just hooked over the toerail. This is fine for a bathing party but a desperate person kicking sideways will unhook it at once. I have seen it happen.

Remember always this question of *buying time.* In a small family cruiser or any cruiser for that matter in which crew strength may be light there is a valuable alternative to the ladder and one of particular importance should the person in the water be heavy and perhaps incapable of huge effort:

it is the inflatable dinghy stowed on the coachroof *half inflated*. The painter must be made fast at its extreme length and the dinghy should have webbing straps holding it which come together to be secured by a single peg or other form of release. If the dinghy is dropped overboard with its forward part inflated it forms a sort of 'dock'. A man can be dragged or drag himself into it and remain there safely prior to the next move. This should always be to get a rope around him so that he cannot possibly be lost.

It is also possible to get a person out of the water by running the mainsail out of its mast track and bundling it over the side to form a sort of sling, still attached to the boom and halyard. If, *if* the person can be dragged into the sling he can be drawn up bit by bit, using the main halyard and the roll of the boat. It can and has been done but only in quiet weather, and it calls for at least three people on deck all of whom know what they are up to.

MAN OVERBOARD AT NIGHT

A person in the water is hard to see even by day. A head is easily hidden in the wave troughs; difficult to pick out among the foam flecks or up-sun against the glitter. He is only visible when both viewer and head are simultaneously on a crest and the urgent necessity to appoint one person as constant watcher cannot be over-stressed. That is by *day*; at night the man in the water cannot be seen at all.

Unless a lifebuoy with attached light lands close to him a searching crew have not a hope in hell (barring lucky chance) of finding him. A powerful torch may scan the water a foot from the man's head and miss him. Or the watcher may see the white gleam of a face among the white gleam of foam and not distinguish one from the other. A light in the water nearby acts as a signpost to the search area but a light on the man's clothing or attached to his person in some way is the only certain way of getting back to him quickly.

There are strobe lights made for just this purpose but they are expensive, not much fun to buy and just one more item to be remembered on watch, ergo they don't get much use. The light on the lifebuoy may be anything from 30 to 100 ft from the man by the time the helmsman has been able to release it in the wake of the yacht and the man may or may not be able to swim to it by the time the yacht returns on her search leg.

In quiet conditions his yells might be heard, or a whistle if it is attached to his lifejacket (if he is wearing one) and if he remembers it is there. In even a moderate sea the surge of water, the clatter and swish of sails and maybe the sound of the engine drowns out a cry for help very easily. The man is at sea level surrounded by as good a sound-deadening system as you could find; moreover a yell heard from a few hundred yards sounds very like a seagull or the squeak of a mainsheet block. To hear anything at all a listening watch needs to be stationed right forward.

Failing a personal light, or a buoy and light dropped instantly, the great problem now is to sail the boat back along her tracks as exactly as possible, using the powerful torch and looking in every direction around the yacht. The task seems, and the odds seem, daunting, but let it be said that there are a great many cases on record of a crew keeping its collective cool, doing just this and saving a life.

It is easy here to set down a set of actions to be taken. None are worth a damn if panic takes over. On a dark night orientation is lost within seconds unless somebody is in level-headed command. The school solution is that the yacht remains on her course heading albeit slowed down by easing sheets, while the person in charge adds or subtracts 180° to obtain a reciprocal course to steer *if she can be held to it*. On a reach she could: hence the desirability of going at once onto a reach and noting the new heading and then when possible sailing the reciprocal. Three things to be done – a reaching course, a new heading and then its reciprocal.

I was once on the helm, in bad weather, when a member of our racing crew went overboard. We were reaching with a preventer guy on the boom. All I could do was yell my head off. Then the skipper came up and took over. We got our man, in the end, but it was touch and go. What I want to stress is that as helmsman and the only one on deck *I would not have been able to cope with* those three things to be done, had I been the skipper of a small family crew; not at once anyway.

I believe that the approach to this emergency must be completely unfettered by rigid drill because every occasion is different. The basics of a drill might be: (1) instantly release a buoy-cum-flag marker, (2) simultaneously yell the alarm, (3) appoint a watcher. Thereafter either slow the boat by letting fly sheets, or reach off noting the course, or gybe all-standing according to what is best at the time. It may be best in light conditions to start the engine at once, maybe drop the headsail and take it from there: *you wouldn't know until it happened.*

Search patterns and equipment A brief panic, confusion, disorientation and there will be good chance that nobody quite knows how far away and in exactly which direction the man lies. We researched this problem on *Yachting Monthly* and evolved a simple search pattern for use at night.

If you know that you are well to leeward of him and must beat back you do so in shallow tacks, counting aloud (Fig. 53A). First tack a count of say ten, second tack a count of twenty, third a count of twenty and so forth: this means that you *should* be tacking for an equal distance either side of the centreline. If you have left him astern on a reach you should gybe, in order to get downwind of the line back. Unless you have a reciprocal compass course to steer you will almost certainly luff above this line if you try to reach back by gauging the course from the wind. Thereafter when it seems certain that you have overshot without finding him

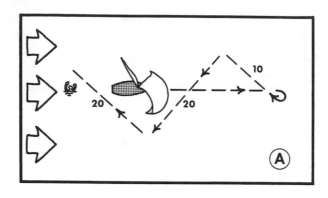

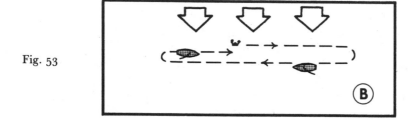

Fig. 53

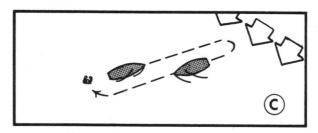

you begin counting on the reach back, *tacking* this time (Fig. 53B). A series of upwind reaches of equal length tacking each time is followed by a series of downwind reaches, gybing each time. If you know for certain that you have got well to windward (perhaps due to holding a closehauled course) the opposite to a tack is a quartering run. If you were on port tack gybe and return with the wind on the starboard quarter (Fig. 53C). Or you proceed downwind on a series of gybing reaches. This is complicated stuff. By the time it appeared necessary, though, it is reasonable to suppose that some sort of calm and composure would have been reached.

Equipment begins with personal buoyancy and harness. If the man isn't wearing either at night the skipper ought to be shot! A lifejacket must have a personal light and a whistle. Equipment for release should make a flag-buoy top priority. It can consist of an 8 ft length of plastic domestic water pipe (not hose) with an expanded polystyrene float and a lead weight 3 ft below the surface and an orange flag plus light-reflective tape. This, carried along the backstay, should be on a quick-release system. At least two lifebuoys should be handy for throwing or release, each with a drogue and at least one of them with a self-activating flashing light. There must be a throwing line or a heaving line (not in a locker) and at all costs a proper boarding ladder which can be secured to the rail firmly. Wire lifelines must have release hooks and spray dodgers must be rigged so that they also can be dropped. Reflective tape (3-M Scotchlite) applied to flag markers, lifebuoys, lifejackets and oilskins shines back with astonishing brilliance in the beam of any powerful electric torch. (See photo section.)

FIRE AFLOAT

I have personally been involved with fire at sea in yachts on three occasions. None proved serious but all three could have been disastrous and all were due to carelessness, my own or others'. An engine fire due to a backfire, an engine room fire due to a bearing running so hot that an oily rag was ignited, and an oil lamp fire.

A yacht is highly combustible whether she be wooden or fibreglass. Prevention of fire is every owner's duty and it boils down to correct installation and disciplined use. The real danger is from explosion, but smoke and toxic fumes from burning synthetics come next.

I will not go deeply into choice of extinguisher because there are plenty of extinguishers specially recommended for use in small yachts. Some are highly effective but give off highly toxic fumes when in contact with fire, others are safe in this respect but may be less effective also. Some extinguishers are all-or-nothing affairs, e.g. once activated you get the whole contents even if the fire is extinguished with the first puff. Others are controllable. There is one curious side issue here; one uses the latter far more willingly knowing that it can be stopped, and a moment of delay wondering whether the fire merits the astonishing mess of a 3 lb dry powder charge may be the crux of the matter.

Ideally there should be three extinguishers. Two big ones of at least 3 lbs capacity each and placed at strategic spots by the engine and forward, away from it, and a third galley extinguisher which can be a small aerosol to deal with fat fires and the like. The common fault and cause of many fires getting out of control is either a miserly provision of extinguishers or extinguishers which are long overdue for replacement or factory overhaul.

Smoke and fumes are a huge problem in all fires. The hotter a fire becomes the more it spreads by raising the temperature of materials which initially don't burn readily, but which burn fiercely once ignition takes place. These produce more fumes. Within a matter of perhaps half a minute the cabin of a small boat can be belching forth huge black billows of dense smoke making it absolutely impossible to get below let alone do anything.

In fighting a fire, then, we must concentrate on the first moment of outbreak. Whether it be a fuel fire or a smoulder which has gone unseen until finally bursting into flame, it must be cooled and starved of oxygen at once. Never fling open a locker or engine box to inspect a suspected fire without having a big extinguisher in your hand and a finger on the firing button. If possible have the second one ready at hand. Open up as little as possible, sweeping the extinguisher jet or powder low down from side to side and smothering the fire. Keep at it. Don't stop to look at the result – smoke may preclude this anyway.

Have somebody turn off the fuel at the main valve, also the gas at the bottle if it happens to be on. Have them draw a bucket of water too for a final dowsing. Don't use water on a fuel fire initially, though, because the burning fuel will float and be spread elsewhere. The whole area must be cooled right down to avoid reignition.

The value of a built-in and possibly automatic sprinkler extinguisher system speaks for itself, otherwise remember that speed is essential and it is vital to regard every fire no matter how apparently insignificant as dangerous.

It will be quickly apparent whether the fire is being controlled. If there is any doubt then immediate steps for abandoning ship must be put in hand by anybody free to do so (we'll deal with this later). A fire in a chip pan may not call for an instant triggering off of the liferaft but even that could become possible.

Where there is a choice and the boat is still under command she must be slowed at once to reduce the flow of air over her. The best angle to the wind may be beam-on in order to carry smoke straight overboard.

A final point about risk of explosion without fire. In the event that somebody smells gas below or petrol fumes, never, *never* turn off any electrical switch or equipment. To do so could cause that vital spark, just as much as switching on. Open up and vent the boat at once.

HOLING AT SEA

Of recent years accounts of attacks by killer whales on ocean cruising yachts and the subsequent sinkings or near-sinkings have brought the problem of a yacht being holed at sea into sharper focus than perhaps the odds on it happening actually merit. For the vast majority of us homicidal whales rate fairly low as a risk of the sea. The risk of being holed by other means is another matter. The biggest risk is floating debris, baulks of timber, steel tanks and the like, and there is a great deal of such stuff floating around at sea. Fortunately most collisions with such flotsom are glancing blows which while they may damage underwater fittings, rudders and propellers seldom do more than scar or crack a hull skin.

How long have we got after being holed? I carried out a small experiment by removing a skin-fitting to leave a $1\frac{1}{2}$ in. diameter hole and then timing a five minute interval; I took in 80 gallons. A typical hand bilge pump with the same diameter intake is rated at 50 gal/min – in other words it would cope easily with a leak of this size provided a small crew was not asked to keep pumping day and night until port was reached.

My 1½ in. hole made an alarming amount of noise and initially the water level appeared to rise at a frightening rate. Note this carefully. A quite modest leak pouring into the narrower area of the bilge appears much more serious than it is; moreover I *knew* how small it was. An emergency leak following a terrific crash and out of reach behind panelling or a GRP interior moulding *and at night* would be a very frightening matter indeed.

Most bilge pumps are of about 12 gal/min capacity although they are obtainable with a 25 gal delivery. In theory such a pump delivery clearing 1500 gal/hr would cope without maximum crew effort, given a leak of my size, but it certainly wouldn't cope with say a 3 in. diameter hole or its equivalent.

A good pump buys precious time. A second man with a bucket might be good for an additional 20–30 gal/min bailing into a self-draining cockpit, but only for a short period, and the cockpit drains would need to be clear. Catching even half a bucketfull in a rolling boat is difficult unless the water is really deep. Unless the leak is so horrifying that water is up to knee depth within the first minute there is a good chance of holding it at bay long enough to staunch it in some way, but the decision is not one to gamble with. Provided there is more than one person aboard, one of them should make ready either the dinghy or the liferaft right away. Then, with an escape route assured, the possibility of dealing with the inrush can be tackled.

Modern GRP yacht construction involving interior mouldings is almost criminally stupid. By tradition, founded on experience a crew should be able to get at the inside of the hull practically everywhere, even at the cost of wrecking interior furniture or panelling. In today's yachts there are whole large areas which are totally inaccessible without proper cutting tools. Since one could not be sure exactly where the leak lay one might wreck half the cabin before finding the right space. There might not be time in any case.

It might be possible to get at the leak from outside and this is the traditional approach in any case. The collision mat is a form of stout sheeting such as canvas which is 'thrummed' or faced with tufts which are sucked into the leak by the inflow of water. The use of such a mat on a round-bodied hull is one thing, the difficulty of lashing it so that it covers a suspected leak when there are fins, skegs, propellers and so forth to cope with, and concave curvature in places, is quite another. Resourceful, ingenious and determined men spurred on by desperation have effected some incredible feats of repair when thousands of miles from land or help. Who knows what we might be capable of doing if the need arose.

There is a big difference between having at least a hope of distress calls being heard and acted upon and being outside all possible hope of immediate help. Bill King, ex-submariner and singlehanding in the Roaring Forties, was holed by an attacking great white shark under the leeside of the hull of his wooden *Galway Blazer II*; he tacked, raising the 2–3 sq ft of splintered damage above water. As long as the breeze held firm to keep the boat heeled, as long as there came neither gale nor calm, he had bought time. He tried the classic trick of 'fothering' a sail over the hole on the outside, which in theory would be sucked into the hole staunching the inrush of water; it couldn't be held taut, in fact it made things worse by scooping up water. In the end he padded and shored up from inside. Eventually, days later and exhausted by pumping, he managed to lash a pad over the hole outside, finally nailing a pair of oilskin trousers to the hull and heaving them fast. Somehow he completed his voyage.

To take two other cases of emergency leakage, one involved a 6 in. hole left by a broken exhaust outlet on the waterline: the crew couldn't even reach the damage and the yacht sank within five minutes. The other case followed striking a rock and then sliding off into deep water with water gushing in on both side of the stern from four separate holes, which the crew tried in vain to pad from within. The yacht sank some quarter of an hour later. In both cases it was apparent from the start that the yacht would have to be abandoned and pumping and repair attempts took second place to the launching and stocking of the liferaft. In both cases all crew survived, thus vindicating their decisions.

To be more realistic, though, and for the modest cruiser not too far from land or help, we are concerned with slowing the leak and delaying the sinking until help might arrive. Every owner must look around his own boat to see how many totally inaccessible parts of the hull he has to contend with, and how they relate to the hull outside. Anywhere else can be coped with by wedging cushions, cramming sleeping bags, towels and so on into lockers containing the leaks or simply appointing someone to *hold* the pad there. Short of damage ripping out a huge area below the waterline, it should be possible to keep a boat afloat long enough to either make port or summon help. If those other areas cannot be dealt with from outside then immediate abandoning may be called for.

Liferafts came in for great criticism following the Fastnet Race tragedy when so many were simply swept away or torn apart by the ferocity of wind and sea. In the case of sinking by holing, a liferaft comes into its own and there can be no substitute in this sort of emergency. No substitute of comparable safety that is. In the absence of a liferaft with its canopy an inflatable dinghy is the next choice in terms of safe flotation. The approved procedure is to keep a grab-bag or panic bag always ready at hand for such an emergency. A big sailbag, perhaps, into which can be thrown the essentials for survival in the open. This means warm protective clothing in bulk, distress signals, torch, repair kit, bellows, water, chocolate, seasickness pills, vital papers and money; but protective clothing with the top priority since death from exposure is a real possibility even in summer should rescue be delayed. Oil-rig type survival suits can now be bought which are lightweight, insulated and fully waterproof. Many lives have already been saved by them. 'Space blankets' are very worth having as they provide heat efficiently, keep off wind and don't soak up water. A panic bag can either be kept half packed as a normal drill on any open-water passage or a crew should be taught what must be put into it.

As an experiment I timed myself in inflating one half of my 8 ft dinghy (at sea it is stowed on deck half-inflated) and launching it, putting the items listed above into a bag and getting afloat. It took a little over six minutes. At night or in bad weather we might call this 12–15 minutes, but perhaps two people very familiar with the yacht might bring it back to around six minutes.

There are many theories concerning stopping leaks and packing a panic bag. Every boat calls for a separate plan but what is really important is that the problem should be considered in advance. A broad outline plan can be evolved:

First phase   Assessment of damage and rate of leak. Cope or abandon?

Second phase   Two people pumping and bailing, third fires distress signals or sends MAYDAY signal, prepares dinghy or raft and grab-bag. OR, if the leak is under control begins moves to reach it and deal with it.

Third phase   Unsuccessful or certain now that the yacht will have to be abandoned. Continue sending distress signals but do *not* use up pyrotechnics if no help is in sight. Aim is to stay with the yacht as long as possible, either aboard or in the raft/dinghy on a slip line. Make every effort to board the raft/dinghy dry-clad.

Much too will depend on the weather. The yacht should be hove-to and left to look after herself, or sails allowed to flog which might attract attention. As she becomes deeper in the water, however, she will lose stability and sails should then be dropped. As a last resort secure the forehatch tightly so that air might be trapped in a pocket forward keeping her afloat for longer.

FOG

Always, fog should be considered an emergency especially in busy waters and in rocky tide-swept regions. With care and cool the real dangers can be reduced or minimised.

We'll take the less dramatic navigational problems first. When fog closes down with the yacht already in an area of fast tidal streams and many rocks, the first essential is to put on the chart the most accurate position it is possible to get, derived from bearings of shore objects and any other sources. If it is possible to strike out for safe open water on a carefully laid and logged course this may be best, provided doing so does not mean heading out into a busy shipping lane. Alternatively if it is possible to reach a safe temporary anchorage this also should be considered.

Otherwise begin a period of painstakingly careful navigation using all available aids including the echosounder. It may also pay to stow sail and proceed slowly under engine. This allows speed through the water to be controlled making for more efficient dead reckoning; also should an area of dangerously breaking water or isolated rocks suddenly appear ahead the yacht can be turned at once without reference to the wind. There is the drawback that engine noise destroys one's hearing and a listener should be stationed forward where he can also operate the foghorn in accordance with the Collision Regulations.

At an early stage try to get some idea of the actual visibility. A ball of newspaper watched as it disappears astern gives some indication but visibility in fog, like sound, is subject to great distortion. Should a mark or buoy appear it is helpful to turn to head the current using the buoy as a guide to stemming the stream in order to estimate its actual rate. I once had the misfortune to be caught in a rocky passage off the west Brittany coast, in a sudden dense fog, a Force 6 wind and a 8 knot tide. I had no idea how strong the current was until a stone tower on a reef appeared close to port and it had a bow-wave like a destroyer!

If under power stop the engine occasionally and listen. There may be land noises, the sound of breakers, engines, hooters and all may be significant in terms of position. In fast tides RDF fixes are not much help due to the time it takes to take the necessary three bearings and plot them. A single good bearing to give a check on a careful DR course possibly checked again by echosounder is a better and safer bet. Be wary of approaching a steep-to and cliff-bound coastline. It is quite possible to sail right into a tiny inlet and not know it until a row of clifftop houses appears above the masthead. On the other hand a gradually sloping seabed fronting a coastline can give a very useful position check, finding a depth contour and then turning to follow it at a safe distance from land.

In quiet weather it is sometimes tempting to consider deep-water kedging, lying perhaps to a very long scope of light warp in 20 fathoms of water safely offshore. If this is done it is vitally important to keep the bell (or any substitute) going and to have a member of the crew on listening watch, ready to slip the anchor and start the engine. Small coasters and fishing boats may well be making a radar run coastwise and a yacht at anchor is the last thing they would be expecting to find. I have heard of two cases of a yacht run down in this way.

The important thing is to find and stay in safe water, not to attempt a port entry unless your position is known to be accurate and to keep as far away from main shipping routes as possible. Fog usually means calm weather, but not always. When there is fog *and* a fresh wind avoid sailing flat out; sail at a speed which provides good control with the least amount of slam and splash. Hearing becomes the vital sense and the less it is impeded the better. Nevertheless regard sound direction and the range of sound with suspicion. The so-called 'lanes of silence' which can exist in fog can make a ship's siren sound to be miles away one moment and right above you the next.

Fog in a shipping lane is another matter. If there is a warning of fog about the only sane thing is to stay out of the shipping lanes but very often we are already in mid-passage when the first warnings of fog are heard on the radio. Ideally we might turn the yacht and make for the nearest easily reached haven reachable without crossing the lanes, or make for shallow water safe from shipping. It is very unlikely that anybody would do this. The instinct is to crack on at full speed in order to clear the lanes before fog closes in and very often it works out that way.

The first thing to do, in daylight at least, is take a long, careful look around the horizon for signs of muzzy visibility. Also noting signs of condensation, a clamminess in the air and perhaps a sharp fall in temperature. At night the lights of shipping may tend to show an aura around them or the fog may be lying in banks and some lights hidden while others remain clear. Plainly it is idiocy to make for and cross a busy lane once fog is well established, but since the combined widths of two lanes and the separation zone between them may add up to 8–10 miles, in some cases it is easy to be caught midway.

Big ships will be having their own problems. One has but to read the many accounts of collision in fog to realize that their radar officers will be disinclined to search for small echoes when collision situations exist all around them. For a yacht to turn and go back may solve nothing. The time spent at risk would be no longer if she pressed on, once halfway across. In a separation system we at least know (or hope) that shipping will be approaching from port or starboard according to the lane we are in. Again, there is little point in motoring dead slow. Cruising speed gives full manoeuvrability. A listening watch right forward will not be disturbed by engine noise; the only problem is that while the skipper may be the best man to have on the helm in case of sudden emergency, he may also be the best listening watch due to his experience.

COLLISION

In fog a ship materializes at incredible speed. It is like watching a photo negative in the developer bath. Within seconds a shape appears, a deepening, a pale blur, then all at once a bow wave and high above it a wall of steel. The sounds she makes materialize in a similar manner. Perhaps it is the rolling roar of her bow wave, or it may be the metallic thump of engines. Often one hears a single clang of metal-on-metal caused by a working party on her deck and occasionally it is the gut-melting bellow of her siren.

Which brings us back yet again to the question of panic. It may not be immediately apparent how the ship is heading, whether she is square-on or coming down at a narrow angle. The yacht helmsman will almost certainly make an instant major helm alteration, probably away from the ship, turning with her, pointing the yachts stern towards her. He may do this quite instinctively and it may or may not be the right thing to do.

An advantage of motoring in fog is that the yacht's radar reflector is less likely to be obscured by her sails and provided it is an effective design the ship may already be turning to avoid collision. It would depend entirely on whether the ship's bridge radar was on a range short enough to detect an echo close ahead, as it might be if conning by nearby channel buoyage. If she is indeed turning there may well be more danger from her stern than from her bow, according to the direction of the turn.

Collision with a much smaller vessel such as a small trawler or coaster may be as dangerous as collision with a big ship. The latter may well push a small yacht aside with her bow wave if the contact is a slanting one. The yacht might be dismasted, engulfed by a wall of water and people could very easily be lost overboard, but unless the ship had a bulbous bow designed to reduce the size of her bow wave and unless she struck exactly square-on there is a good chance of survival. A smaller vessel would roll her under and smash the hull; also her helmsman might be the only man on watch and not equal to the occasion.

Let us suppose that the yacht is motoring at 4–5 knots in calm and fog with visibility at perhaps 50–200 yards. Suddenly everybody is yelling and pointing. They may not see the vessel's upperworks at all let alone the angle of her masts which would indicate her heading. The bow wave might be an indication. If it was a symmetrical shape like a pair of flaring wings it could indicate that she was square-on, but viewed from a little to one side or the other these wings would appear lopsided. This theory goes awry if the ship should be breasting a sea which was coming from a beam-on direction.

The time remaining for avoiding action could be as little as 10 seconds. Stop reading and look at the sweep hand of your watch while mentally visualizing that first glimpse and the time taken to slam your helm over. The comforting fact seems to be that one hears of far more near misses and side-swipes than one does of fatal run-downs (Fig. 54).

In fog, among shipping, everybody should be wearing lifejackets fitted with whistles and harnesses should *not* be used. An aerosol foghorn (provided it works in dense fog, and quite often the reed freezes as the gas meets it and only a small squark is produced) is also a good thing to have in hand. The inflatable dinghy should be towed on a slip-hitch with one person in charge of it and if there is a liferaft aboard it should be ready for instant automatic action, again, in the charge of one person. Crew should remain on deck for so long as danger exists or remain below fully clad and ready to be called up.

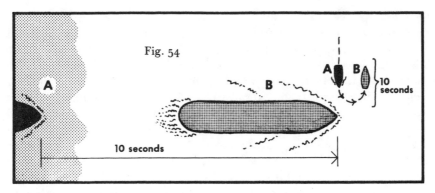

Reconstruction of a narrow miss. Ten seconds has elapsed between when the ship and the yacht were at A and when they are at B.

In the event of collision and sinking there is no guarantee of being picked up quickly – or for that matter of the ship's crew even being aware that a small yacht had been run down. Survival in the water after collision would also depend upon whether the propellers could be avoided, whether the ship was deep or lightly laden. Supposing that the catastrophe did happen and that it was seen, the ship might carry her way for half a mile or even more before she could be stopped and turned around. An emergency call would be made to other ships and rescue services and *in time* the area would be searched. For those in the water it would be their whistles and the ability to stand immersion that would then count. This is where the inflatable or the raft could be so vital. People must be kept close together, they should not exercise their limbs to keep warm but remain as quiet as possible. The subject of survival is a vast one and worth separate study.

DRAGGING ANCHOR

Although this is not an emergency unless it is a factor leading to a more tangible danger it must be included in this cheery chapter.

The classic danger situation would be in dragging onto a dangerous lee shore during heavy weather, which might lead to the total loss of the yacht. A lesser risk, but perhaps leading to heavy costs, would be dragging onto other yachts lying to leeward. A dangerous lee shore could be a sea wall, rocky beach, steep-to surf-bound beach or a sandbank open to breaking seas. A mud shore in a sheltered river is not a dangerous lee shore, merely an embarrassing one.

The assumption must be that the yacht has veered all the cable she has be it rope or chain but is still dragging either because the holding was poor in the first place or the water too deep, due maybe to a high range of tide and high water, or for some other reason. It must also be assumed that the anchor is heavy enough for the vessel, in which case it has probably collected kelp weed, a tin can on the point, taken a foul hitch in its own cable or suffered some other such impediment. It must also be assumed that it is blowing at gale force or thereabouts.

The first considerations are how fast is she dragging and how near is the lee shore (or other boats to leeward)? Next, is the wind a passing squall associated with a rapidly moving front or is it an established blow likely to continue for some hours at least? If she is dragging steadily and slowly can we be certain that she will continue at the same rate? An anchor can break out as it passes over a seabed gully or over a deeper area, losing its tenuous hold completely. How long do we have before the danger to leeward becomes unavoidable?

There are the obvious remedies. The engine can be run at half speed and a second anchor can be let go. If the engine is used to take weight off the cable the helm must be manned because there will be lulls in the wind when she will forge ahead then pay off at an angle. The return of the next squall would then set her back on her anchor with such a jerk that in the end the engine, if left unattended, may do more harm than good.

The use of a second anchor bears out once again that it should be an anchor only slightly lighter than the main bower and not a baby kedge. By all means a baby kedge as well, since one cannot have too many anchors (as Saint Paul found, Acts xxvii), but a second anchor which was too light in weight would only add a complication. Since the main cable would be fully out there would be no chance to bend on a second anchor to that same cable. Neither could it be bent on to the bower so that the two anchors worked in tandem. It would have to be laid separately from the bow, paying out scope to it as the yacht dragged and taking the strain when scope enough had been veered. Or, by sheering off-line under engine the second anchor could be laid so that the yacht laid in the centre of the V. The former might be better since when laid in a V the natural sheering of the yacht would put weight first on one and then the other separately, probably dragging each by turn. With both in line ahead the main strains should be shared more evenly.

The use of anchor weights referred to earlier might prevent dragging in the first place and might stop it once it had started by cushioning the snubbing which is the first cause of dragging, but the crew would feel very insecure thereafter. They would want to get clear altogether, either to find some other anchorage or go to sea in search of better shelter farther down the coast. Recovering an anchor in a gale is no easy matter.

The vital thing is to decide earlier rather than later that the anchor must be recovered and the boat got under way. Once the danger is a few lengths to leeward the only safe course might be to slip the whole lot, leaving it buoyed for later recovery, and clear out under engine. The consequences of heading to sea without an anchor other than the kedge need no explanation. You would have to be very sure of engine, sails and crew to consider it a safe expedient.

To begin with, the anchor would have to be recovered by motoring up on it. The bows would be rearing and smashing down. The foredeck party would have to haul in cable fast and be ready to take a turn like greased lightning as the yacht sheered and laid her weight into it. She would likely over-run it. The anchor despite dragging might be very firmly embedded or heavy with collected kelp. The foredeck would be a very dangerous place indeed. When the anchor finally broke the bows would most probably sheer off wildly downwind trailing maybe 4–5 fathoms of cable and anchor which the foredeck party were struggling to haul in. If she was very close to the lee shore it would be very much a matter of engine power whether the helmsman could get her head-to-wind in time to begin punching out towards safety. The additional weight on the foredeck in a smallish cruiser could well bring the stern up and cause the propeller to cavitate in thin water or even break surface altogether.

In dragging down onto other anchored yachts the risks of total loss are less but the complications are formidable. By use of engine and helm the dragging yacht could be sheered aside and so prevent actual collision – at first. If she continues to drag she will ultimately foul somebody else's anchor and cable on the seabed and then the band will begin to play!

Either she will cause this anchor to drag also, with both yachts now descending upon the next boat to leeward, or her anchor will run up the cable of the luckless stranger until our own yacht is lying astern and both then drag in tandem. With this sort of mix-up and with a sea running any attempt at recovering one's anchor will simply means both yachts being brought into shattering contact and greatly endangering crew who attempt to separate or fender off the hulls. The only answer is to let slip and run clear.

Letting slip an anchor is not always easy. Chain is usually in one length or if not then it is joined by means of patent shackles or joining links which are not easy to open even in calm conditions. Using a hacksaw is out because it takes too long. The whole lot must be let go.

The best provision for this is to secure the bitter end of the chain to the chain locker below by means of a 1 fathom length of synthetic fibre rope, which will permit a knot small enough to be drawn up through the navel pipe on deck. The chain end can then be buoyed quickly by attaching a fender by means of a heaving line (lead this back in from the bow fairlead to do so, thus allowing the fender to remain outboard and removing the risk of its fouling as it might if it had to follow the disappearing chain end out through the fairlead), and then cut the fathom length just prior to casting off the chain completely.

The yacht is now adrift. One problem overcome and the next a test of seamanship. Such an incident occuring in a river could mean that we now have a yacht unable to anchor and unable to find a mooring, scudding around under engine in a gale-swept river looking for somewhere to go. If all else fails there is one safe alternative – safe provided the river banks are flat and muddy. She can be run ashore on the weather side and beached. This is contrary to a seaman's entire nature but it just could be the wise, cheapest and safest decision. I have never yet had to recourse to this but neither is it ever far from my thoughts in this sort of situation.

We have assumed throughout that the yacht will be handled under engine. If the engine is unreliable or low-power we have a very different state of affairs. If for instance it lacks the guts to motor up on the anchor to recover it, then it will have to be motor-sailed out (see Anchoring chapter), under the deepest possible reef and the smallest possible headsail or none at all for preference. Recovering the cable would be very hairy indeed. Moreover, once broken out, only the mainsail would enable the yacht to get her bows up into the wind.

In slipping the cable and running off downwind it could be more sensible to stow the mainsail and have a headsail ready to be jerked aloft as a means of turning her head downwind very quickly. With an unreliable rather than a merely weak engine the demands on seamanship are much greater. At every stage of an operation the skipper must have in mind what to do if it stops on him and the crew forward must be ready on the instant to let go anchor again. Above all the skipper must never let the situation deteriorate by leaving things too late. He must get the hell out just as soon as it is plain that his anchor on full scope is not going to hold.

DISMASTING

For what is surely a spectacular emergency the loss of the mast is usually no threat to the crew at the time it happens. For whatever reason it fails, it seems to go quite gently and by reason of the thrust imparted by the sails being forward it almost always falls well clear of the cockpit. There are exceptions: in one case a man below had but newly quit the lavatory seat when the deck-stepped mast jumped its step, pierced the deck and shattered the pan to dust beside him!

The mast may remain undamaged but this is rare. A buckling spreader or a vital shroud parting means instant gross distortion of the spar and then breakage, often aloft but usually bringing down the whole spar.

The immediate worry is how long the yacht can afford to lie helpless. At all costs if the mast is over the side the skipper must resist starting the engine until all wires and ropes are brought back aboard. It is likely to take several hours at least before the ship can be brought back under any sort of control and if she is going to drift into danger sooner than that the skipper must consider sending out distress signals. Not otherwise, provided the weather is not also a factor, because it is within the ability of a crew in a yacht with a good engine to get themselves out of the mess.

Dismantling rigging is a major problem. Bottlescrew forks may be bent and pins distorted. There may only be a meagre choice of tools aboard. Needed will be enough spanners, grips or/and pliers plus a hacksaw for a couple of people to work at the dismantling while others heave and sort the tangle of wires and cut free the sail slides from the mast. In the least seaway the now rapid and jerky motion will make the job much more difficult. Sails over the side and filled with water take time to free and recover and a metal mast also now full of water does not float, in fact it becomes impossible to lift unless the head can be raised first allowing the water to drain out at the break. Heavy-duty wire or bolt cutters are the swift answer to dismantling a mast, but understandably a skipper who will have to fork out for a new set of rigging will prefer to salvage all he can even if only the fittings.

Getting the mast back on deck is no light task and it may pay to remove the lifelines for the whole length of the boat on one side, or to make a gap so that the spar can be hauled forward and then aft where it can be lashed down on a bed of cushions or fenders to protect the deck. The aim then will be to continue under engine, making for the nearest safely entered haven. Do NOT fire distress signals if all you are after is a tow. A distress signal says clearly and in law that you consider your ship to be in danger and this lays you wide open to a salvage claim later.

If you do come across a fishing boat, for instance, make it absolutely clear that you are contracting for a tow and if possible get it agreed in writing or at least fully witnessed. Use your own towrope if possible but if the best you have is clearly inadequate, use his rope but secure it at your end yourself. Beware the bossy professional or yachtsman who tries to take full command. A salvage claim can be made to stick if it can be shown that but for the salvor's efforts the yacht was likely to have been lost. Agree a towage fee and don't be mean. An insurance company worth its salt will accept this debt. Remember also that a towage job can turn into a salvage job if for instance the weather becomes dangerous and the yacht could plainly not have got herself off a dangerous lee shore (or suchlike) unaided. A court decides 'what is reasonable', which may or may not be to your benefit.

JURY MASTS

Like the pea and thimble or the three-card trick, the theory of the jury mast is far simpler than the practice. The aim is to erect any sort of spar tall enough to spread enough canvas to offer running or reaching progress at sufficient speed to make it all worthwhile.

If a stump of a keel-stepped mast remains the task is easier, but most masts are deck-stepped and any sort of pole raised on end must be fully stayed and braced as it is lifted. On a jerking, rolling boat this calls for careful measurement and long and carefully planned preparation. Better is to utilise two spars in an A form. Even if they are of different lengths, by lashing them to bring the top of the taller over the middle of the deck the added stability of this form makes it a first choice. Only two stays in a fore-and-aft direction are then needed and by providing a block at the head a third spar (if one can be found) can be raised to extend the height of the sail still farther (Fig. 55).

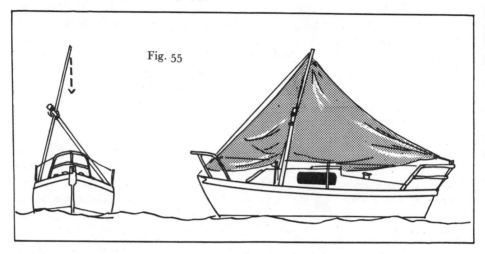

Fig. 55

The sail set then depends on the height achieved. A headsail can be hoisted by its clew or a corner of a spinnaker, with broom and boathook extending the lower parts, or the head of the mainsail, or even a squaresail improvised from a cockpit awning. It is very difficult to effect even the simplest of rigs unless conditions are very quiet, and in a prolonged calm it would be an act of hope rather than one of urgent necessity.

The reason for attempting a jury rig is perhaps more pressing. Lacking radio and with some hundreds of miles to go it would be an obvious need; food doesn't last forever and a ship would only be able to rescue the yacht's crew. The need may be to avoid a dangerous area to leeward by reaching clear of it, or it may be a simple matter of having run out of fuel with safe haven a short distance away. There is one more good reason though. To be able to get the yacht home or to safety without howling to be rescued is something to be proud of in these times, when the tendency to send up flares for every little contingency is so widespread.

WRECK

There is an obvious difference between stranding and wreck, the latter implying that the hull is so damaged that the yacht is no longer seaworthy. That simple stranding can easily become wreck is obvious and sadly this is often the case. A yacht might ground on a reef or sandbar on a falling tide but in a rising wind. Her crew might then have a wait of up to 12 hours (depending on the state of the ebb when she went on) during which time her plight might have become very serious indeed. The same could be true of running onto a rock and damaging the rudder – no immediate danger but a potential of very real problems when she next floated. These waiting hours are critical in terms of what the crew can do to either get stand-by help or to prepare to help themselves.

The sandbar situation might call for laying out to windward the best anchor on the longest scope it is possible to make up. The aim here is not merely holding power but hauling off. There might be a heavy breaking sea if the bank was steep, or a long series of smaller seas to haul off through. The yacht's bilge might take severe punishment while beginning to lift on the new flood and thereafter risk her rudder as she began to pitch heavily – if it was like so many of today's rudders and vulnerable to striking the ground. A good engine would be the best insurance but initially the propeller would be churning too near the surface much of the time as she pitched (Fig. 56).

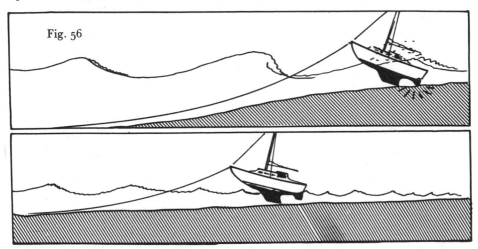

Fig. 56

Rudder damage, in anything but calm conditions on the returning tide, would demand that a satisfactory jury rudder had been contrived during the wait. It isn't much use detailing methods of construction because it must vary for every case, depending on materials available. There is a difference, though, between a system for holding a boat straight on course and a rudder which will allow her to be manoeuvred. A towed spar or a bucket from the end of the boom can be made to work in the former case, but some form of big paddle is needed in the latter. The main boom might be the longest available spar. It can be given a fulcrum, albeit a sloppy one, by means of cross-lashing between the stanchions of the after pulpit, if they are very strongly bolted, and locker fronts or floorboards might be used to fabricate a paddle blade, sandwiching the end of the boom and drilling and bolting two boards (one either side) so that it is in effect a double blade. Cabin sole boards, the heads door or whatever is handy and suitable should be used. The gamble is that there can be no trial and error. It has to be right first time (Fig. 57).

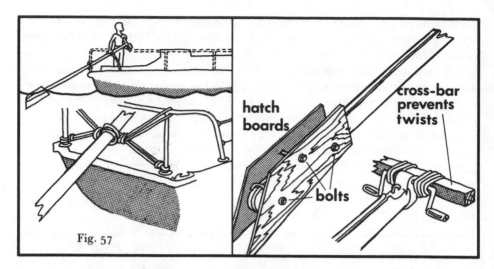

Fig. 57

hatch boards

bolts

cross-bar prevents twists

If a yacht is wrecked and holed so badly that only the rock prevents her from sinking the skipper has a big and fast decision to take. She might go on with an almighty crash and water might begin flooding in below. There would follow a series of rending crashes. A skipper might be forgiven for instinctively doing all in his power to *get off the rocks*.

The points raised earlier under holing at sea apply with regard to the size of the hole and the volume of water entering. It is totally unrealistic to say that a skipper in this predicament should blithely opt to hold his boat on the rocks so that she can't sink. In any case hitting could happen on a rising tide. If it happens on the ebb, with deep water all around the matter is very different. By allowing the boat to sink on the rocks much of the pounding would be lessened but equally, much more damage would result in the process. This is one of those cases for getting important priorities in their right order. If we float off into deep water are we likely to sink quickly and are we beyond reach of land? If we stay here will we be safer despite the certainty of worse damage to the boat?

There are so many factors to consider. Does the rock dry out completely? What is the weather doing? Is help available? Is the sea rough or is she merely bumping and grinding quite lightly, and so on. Safety of human life comes first. Take steps to safeguard it and then consider the boat.

RESCUE BY SHIP OR HELICOPTER

If there is any chance at all of the crew of a sinking or otherwise distressed yacht being taken off, at sea, by a big ship one rule is paramount: all MUST WEAR SAFETY HARNESS as well as lifejackets of course.

It is all-important that rescuers have a reliable strongpoint to grab hold of or indeed to lift people by. There have been many cases of survivors faced with a long vertical climb up a swaying ladder while weak from exhaustion and fear who just stuck halfway, or fell, or refused to climb at all. In all these cases had it been possible to attach a line to a harness they would have climbed with little trouble, feeling secure and helped from above.

Rescue by big ship at sea more often than not means either the dismasting of the yacht or abandoning her, or both. There is no way in which a big ship can tow a yacht at a speed commensurate with the safety of the yacht and the management of the ship, nor has a shipmaster that sort of time to spare unless perhaps his ship is a small coaster or fishing vessel. To lie alongside for taking off crew means almost always extensive damage, especially if the yacht gets underneath an overhanging bow or stern. There is also a big danger of crew being crushed by falling between the two hulls. The ship would make a lee, or steam very slowly with the yacht partly in her lee, and crew might be taken off by a number of means including a lowered cargo net, a lift cage, a lowered boat or the pilot ladder. There might be an entry door lower in the hull. Whatever the method, the combined movements of the two hulls would produce a vertical movement of maybe 12 ft depending on the swell. The ship would probably lower a crewman to supervise but the difficulties are great and should be considered before asking for assistance of this kind.

By their own admission big-ship men today (unless they are spare time yachtsmen) know very little about yachts in terms of their strength, speed, handling or equipment. Naval personnel are different. Not only have they a good deal of small boat experience but they are trained in the rescue of survivors from the water, and naval vessels are far more manoeuvrable than most merchantmen. Fishing crews and boats share this to a great extent. The sight of a huge tanker seems to offer immediate refuge to the distressed crew of a small yacht but the scruffy little drifter may be a far more realistic option if there is any choice in the matter.

Rescue by the lifeboat service means rescue by experts – who will also try to save the yacht as well. Even so, much can be done to make their job easier. A yacht aground and breaking up could help things if the crew streamed their dinghy to leeward to be picked up from it by a lifeboat which might not be able to get closer. Or if a line-throwing rocket was used and the yacht skipper knows how to haul in and secure the breeches-buoy gear. A skipper is as much in command of his yacht when she is a wreck as at any other time and he must be able to organize and think for his crew.

Helicopter rescue also means abandoning the yacht, but if she is otherwise intact she may well be salvaged at sea. The essentials of helicopter rescue are as follows.

The lift wire will be lowered into the sea to discharge static. A crewman will then descend on it. Unless the yacht has a bare area of deck which offers no risk of the wire fouling and possibly even crashing the aircraft, the survivors will have to be lifted from the water. ON NO ACCOUNT MUST THE WIRE EVER BE MADE FAST.

Survivors will be required to take to the water in lifejackets, one at a time, or alternatively the dinghy or liferaft may be streamed downwind on a painter with the crew aboard. Sails should be taken down and lashed on deck pending the downdraft from the helicopter rotors. If a sick person is being sent up and nobody from the yacht can be spared to go with him, details of his symptoms, treatment, drugs given and when, time of injury or onset of illness, time when tourniquet was last loosened, *any* known previous medical conditions (such as diabetes, heart trouble, allergies, epilepsy), etc must go with him in the form of a note. Don't forget his name, home address and phone number and whom to contact ashore.

There is a signal used by helicopters at night, a green flare, which indicates that the casualty has been seen and the helicopter is turning, and the yacht's crew should wait until this flare has died away before firing further red flares. This is important because the aircrew, in order to preserve night vision, will not look out while the green flare is burning and thus would not see the red flare (which could well be the last one in stock) marking the yacht's position.

Prior to this a yacht crew must take pains to make it very obvious that they are the yacht in need of help. If all flares have been used up (and at least a couple should always be saved for recognition use) Morse code signals by torch at night, the use of dye markers by day, or deliberately 'odd' behaviour will tell the rescuers what the need to know. Odd behaviour can be the lowering of sails halfway, or allowing them to fall over the side, or (a recognized signal) waving both arms up and down while outstretched to the sides.

There is a good deal to learn about rescue by helicopter but in the distress of the moment it is enough to remember the essentials and let the aircraft crew take full charge.

TOWING AT SEA

Many of the emergencies dealt with throughout the foregoing chapter may end up by the yacht being towed. We have glanced quite briefly at the implications of salvage. The saving of the yacht and crew take first priority.

Securing a towline is the first problem and an owner's failure to do this properly is the reason that the tow skipper so often has to interfere. Few yachts have adequate bitts or deck cleats for an open-sea tow. Even if it is strong and large enough it could tear half the foredeck out in a lightly constructed yacht. Nor can the base of a deck-stepped mast be used since it is engineered to take a compression rather than a lateral load.

Plainly the foredeck cleats or bitts will be tried first. The towline must be lead through the bow fairlead and *lashed* into it so that if the yacht takes a wild sheer it will not jump out and maybe part the forestay. If the yacht has anchor chain it is no bad plan to secure the towline to the chain and pay out perhaps 15 fathoms to act as a damper by reason of its weight. In heavy conditions yachts have been towed this way but leaving the anchor on as well to help preserve this snatch-damping catenary.

If the towing skipper knows his job he will start off very slowly, turning the yacht in a wide circle until on course and never snatching her bows around from right angles. The helmsman of the yacht must follow exactly in the wake of the tow boat, doing all he can to minimize snatch and shock. Usually the towline should remain in the water of its own weight, perhaps rising out of it by a foot or so only on the peak loads.

EXERCISES

Emergencies call for quick thinking and quick action. The more one can think in advance the more likelihood there is that we will think and act correctly in an emergency. The aim should be to ensure that at least two people in the regular crew (skipper and mate?) should have shared this advance thinking and have detailed knowledge of equipment, the boat, and any standing orders or simple drills that may be evolved.

The philosophy of safety should not be made a grim and finger-wagging matter. Viewed constructively, safety considerations in cruising do not limit one's pleasure and cast a sour and sombre cloud over the activities, but quite the reverse. The safer a boat and crew become, the more they can do. In a safely run boat there is less apprehension and more confidence.

The rest of the watch keeping crew, whether regular or occasional members, should not be excluded from plans and deliberations and they should certainly know as much about them as their ages and experience allow. The techniques of safety are techniques like any other form of seamanship and should be treated as such. The casual question posed over the breakfast table, 'Who knows where the extinguishers live and who knows how to work them?' may well surprise everybody – and reveal a huge gap in everybody's knowledge.

EXERCISE 1   Crew knowledge

Ask and discover how many aboard know:
1. How to find and use distress signals
2. How many fire extinguishers on board; where they are
3. How to start the engine
4. How to use VHF or whatever other radio is fitted
5. How to launch and activate the liferaft, if any
6. How to throw a line.

Organize a 'Safety Sail'. This could well form a joint club outing. Crews can be taken through the theories and simple drills which each skipper may evolve for dealing with man overboard, fire, abandoning ship etc. Demonstrations might also be arranged (flares, liferafts, etc) and the

Coastguard asked to send an officer to talk to crews. If a fire extinguisher is due for renewal or overhaul (well, is it?) a fire demonstration ashore can be arranged under guidance of a safety officer from the Fire Service.

EXERCISE 2   Fire

List fire hazards in your own boat. Careless use of gas cooker, pilot lights, sparking electrics, smokers, exhaust systems, fuel stowage and fuel lines, et al. List most flamable and otherwise dangerous material on board (distress flares, various fabrics, foam cushions or mattresses), personal belongings (aerosol spray cans, for instance), paint, resin and solvents, etc.

Review fire appliances: age, size, type, adequacy. Remember the bucket. Base a crew drill on the following considerations. Extinguisher ready before opening up fire to the air. Crew out. Aim low, sweep to and fro. Exclude air, hold your breath. Second extinguisher ready at hand. Cut off piped fuel and gas supply, as close to the source as possible as well as at the 'use' end of the line. Boat stopped to reduce draught effect of wind. Crew ready to abandon. Make absolutely sure that the fire is out and the site is cool.

EXERCISE 3   Man overboard

Attach a weight to a plastic fender so that it will float about upright but will not drift too fast in the wind. Run through the following manoeuvres for the benefit of crew and allow each individual to have a shot at them.
On the run : harden up closehauled and tack to approach buoy from leeward.
Closehauled : demonstrate difference between (a) an instant gybe and luff; (b) a gybe after a 20 second delay.
Reaching : continue until boat can be turned. Return and slow boat to leeward by trimming sails.
Recover the buoy and put it into a grey, green or other harder-to-see plastic bag. Drop it and appoint crew to spot it as you sail away. Go down-sun if the sun is bright.

EXERCISE 4

You need a good swimmer in a lifejacket or flotation jacket who will deliberately 'fall' overboard by secret arrangement. Choose a time when the regular crew are relaxed, having tea as you sail along. Choose safe, open water and conditions in which you will be able to take over if necessary and guarantee his safe recovery. This sounds both risky and unwise. Man overboard is a very serious emergency and the exercise will bring home to everybody just how difficult it is in *fine* weather, let alone bad weather, to recover a heavy person from the water.

EXERCISE 5

Study the search patterns for night emergency. By giving a helmsman a pair of smoked (welder's) goggles to wear to simulate restricted night vision the value of systematic search is demonstrated.

EXERCISE 6   Abandoning ship

As a likely emergency this seems so remote and unlikely that a crew cannot be expected to take it very seriously and it is unfair to labour the point.

As skipper, the thinking is very much in your domain. Cockpit conversation while sailing gently along is probably the best form of crew education. Pose the question: given five minutes' grace and a big sailbag what would you stuff into it? Warmth (dryness), fresh water and the means of signalling by day or night should top the list. Also how fast can we inflate the dinghy?

EXERCISE 7   Holing

Make a sketch plan of the hull inside, beginning at the bow and detailing areas of hull which cannot be inspected or reached without ripping away interior moulding or panelling. Consider whether a large inrush of water would be able to drain aft to the bilge pump. Whether it would have to reach serious proportions before it would drain aft over and around floors and lockers.

Check the volume capacity of the pump. Try pumping at the maximum rate necessary to achieve this by flooding the bilge sufficiently. How long could it be kept up? Is the pump really man enough?

Consider the practicalities of bucket bailing from bilge into self-draining cockpit. Will the drains keep up with the quantity of water? How many buckets or gallons could you shift per minute and hope to keep it up?

EXERCISE 8   Fog

Afloat on a still, calm day. Close your eyes and listen. Note the degree of noise made by the yacht (sails swishing, water, gear rattling etc) and find the spot on deck offering the best listening place for other outside noises. Note the distance at which ship's engines, bow wash, other sounds can be heard and the effect of wind direction. Identify shore sounds as a means of navigational confirmation. If it is possible to find a place on the bare hull inside the boat, below the waterline, against which you can press your ear, listen for nearby bell buoys or submarine signals, propeller beat and so on.

EXERCISE 9   Ship shapes in fog

Much of modern shipping looks more like a block of flats than a vessel at sea; Ro-Ros, container ships, ferries in particular make baffling silhouettes. Take particular note of the outline shapes of ships from various angles and distances. Photograph them for later study. Try to decide in every case which features give an indication of the course angle. Pay particular attention to bow wave sizes and shapes according to type of bow, type and size of ship, and state of lading.

Speed. Watch shipping as it comes up to and passes an offshore buoy. Fix your eye on a point in the water a short distance ahead of a ship and guess how many seconds will elapse before she reaches it (you can do this just before she reaches a buoy). Time by counting aloud 'One thousand two thousand three thousand etc etc'. This little exercise is always a surprise: ships travel faster than one realizes.

EXERCISE 10   Dismasting

Check the ship's toolbox for spanners of a size suitable for releasing rigging screw nuts, and non-rusty pliers for removing split pins. Provide a full-size hacksaw and at least a dozen spare blades including high-speed tungsten for tackling stainless steel. Measure boom and spinnaker pole with a view to making an A-frame jury mast. How high would it be at the apex? Could a third spar be improvised to use as a yard to raise a corner of a headsail still higher?

Jury rudder Consider ways and means of using the main boom as a big steering paddle, as detailed earlier; or the spinnaker pole if long enough. Having thought out a feasible plan that seems likely to work, ensure that the necessary drills, bolts, lashing line and wire and other requirements are aboard. It may well be that the addition of a couple of powerful G-clamps would make it possible to use a saloon door or the hatchboards. Think it out.

EXERCISE 11   Rescue

Buy (if you don't have them) International Code flags **F** (I am disabled; communicate), **O** (Man overboard), **V** (I require assistance), **W** (I require medical assistance), and **NC** (Distress). Buy the largest available for yachts.

Understand the following Priority calls, on radio:
MAYDAY = Distress, in grave and imminent danger
PAN = Urgent message concerning safety
SECURITE = Station is about to transmit message concerning safety of navigation or weather warning.

If possessing RT study the full instructions for making distress calls and requesting assistance.

Plan to use pyrotechnics as follows. Red flares and smoke: up to 3 miles offshore or when in plain sight of shipping or aircraft. Up to within 7 miles of the coast or when low cloud prohibits use of rockets: 2-star red signals. Over 7 miles, use red parachute rockets.

Signals can of course be used in any order but the above makes the best use of them in terms of range. It is thought best to use pyrotechnics in pairs. Thus a watcher might imagine he had seen a signal but be uncertain; a second fired perhaps one minute later would receive his full attention. Red flares are also to be used as a means of guiding a rescuer to the scene. Do not use all the stocks at once; save at least one rocket and four red flares.

Coastguard Yacht and Boat Safety Scheme

The U.K. Coastguard issues a post-paid card upon which an owner can record a description of his boat and her distinguishing features. This is filed against the possibility of her becoming reported as missing. A phone call to the nearest CG station prior to a passage and another call or communication via VHF Channel 16 on arrival or if plans are changed ensures that you are under watch for that period.

The Coastguard also advises leaving full details of your boat, radio callsign, fuel range, cruise/passage plans, and all crew names and addresses with a reliable person ashore.

Appendix One – Notes on the Text

CHAPTER II – HANDLING UNDER POWER

DISTANCE JUDGING

The following criteria apply to people with average eyesight.

50 yards:	Faces appear blurred but plainly recognizable.
100 yards:	Faces reduced to dots for eyes and mouth. Main yacht details identifiable, shop names may be legible.
200 yards:	Faces seen as pale blurs, roof slates distinguishable, clinker planking visible in good light.
400 yards:	Movement of figures detectable, oars in rowing boat, etc. Faces invisible, main rigging just visible in good light.
500 yards:	Human figure seen as a small dash. Crossbars on windows and window shape just visible.
1 mile:	Large buoy shapes identifiable; big ships' portholes and house windows still have shape. Human figures if seen at all become dots.
2 miles:	Windows become dots, small buoys not seen and large ones lose their shape. Human figures not seen.
3 miles:	Big-ship bow wave visible from average cockpit height, also waves breaking on a beach.
4 miles:	Trees, hedges etc are blurred shapes and all colours becoming greyish. Bow waves and shore waves not seen from average cockpit.

CHAPTER VI – ANCHOR WORK

WEIGHT OF ANCHOR

In any table of recommended weights the safe rule is to choose an anchor weight nearer to the top of the scale. In the table below a 22 ft boat needs a 17 lb CQR and a 28 ft boat a 30 lb CQR, for example: it would be foolish to assume that a 17 lb anchor would be suitable for anything larger than 22 ft. A 25 lb anchor should be chosen for say a 24-footer. In the course of history thousands of ships have been lost because their anchors were a little under weight and thousands saved because they were just a little over weight.

Length		Chain only link diam.		Nylon warp circ. diam.		CQR or Danforth	
ft	*m*	*in*	*mm*	*in.*	*mm*	*lbs*	*kg*
22	6.7	$\frac{1}{4}$	6.3	$1\frac{1}{2}$	12	17	8
28	8.5	$\frac{5}{16}$	8	$1\frac{3}{4}$	14	30	14
35	10.7	$\frac{3}{8}$	9.5	2	16	35	16
41	12.5	$\frac{3}{8}$	9.5	$2\frac{1}{4}$	18	43	20
49	14.9	$\frac{7}{16}$	11	$2\frac{1}{2}$	20	55	25

It should be remembered that overall length in feet takes no account of special windage problems. One 28-footer can be of low profile and with a low-windage modern rig, while another boat of equal length can be designed with high freeboard, a wheelhouse and a heavily rigged mast. It is windage allied to sheering and snubbing that puts the heaviest strains on an anchor.

RELATING ECHO SOUNDER TO CHART SOUNDINGS

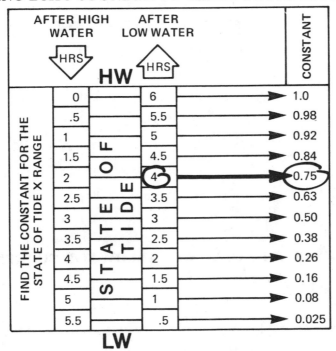

For instance, the chart shows a 4 metre patch and it's 4 hours after Low Water. If we're on the patch what should the echosounder be reading? Find the Range for that day from tide tables or, approximately, by taking the local Rise for the day × 2 minus Local Spring Rise = Range. Consult the table here.

RANGE = DAY'S RISE × 2 − SPRING RISE

Example: Range for the day is 5 m. The table shows that for 4 hours after Low Water the Constant is 0.75. Multiply × 5 = 3.75 m. You should have roughly 3.75 m extra on that 4 m patch, and the echosounder should therefore read 7.75 m (depth from the surface).

If it is a period of neap tides the Low Water level will be somewhat above the Chart Datum of 4 m on the patch and Range must be subtracted from the day's Rise: e.g. day's Rise 5.5 m − Range of 5.0 m = 0.5 + 7.75 = 8.25 m.

CHAPTER VII – PILOTAGE

SPEED AND DISTANCE: LAYING OFF FOR TIDE

These tables give rough approximations, suitable for kneecap navigation over short distances.

Examples: At 3 knots a boat will sail 2 miles in 40 minutes.

At 4 knots with a 1 knot tidal set 45° on bow or quarter the yacht should be headed up into the tide 10°.

At 2 knots with 1 knot of tide on the beam she would have to be headed up 30°.

SPEED, TIME AND DISTANCE

Distance Travelled (N.M.)

SPEED	1	2	3	4	5	6
1 kn	1h	2h	3h	4h	5h	6h
2 kn	30m	1h	1h 30	2h	2h 30	3h
3 kn	30m	40m	1h	1h 20	1h 40	2h
4 kn	15m	30m	45m	1h	1h 15	1h 30
5 kn	12m	24m	36m	48m	1h	1h 12
6 kn	10m	20m	30m	40m	50m	1h

COURSE ALTERATION TO ALLOW FOR CURRENT

Current 45° on Bow or Stern

1	2	3	4	5	6	Boat Speed (knots)		CURRENT on the Beam					
								1	2	3	4	5	6
20°	10°	7°	5°	4°	3°	½	½	30°	15°	10°	8°	6°	5°
45°	20°	13°	10°	8°	6°	1	1		30°	20°	15°	12°	10°
	32°	20°	15°	12°	10°	1½ Tidal Rate (knots)	1½			30°	22°	18°	15°
	45°	28°	20°	16°	14°	2	2				30°	23°	20°
		36°	26°	20°	17°	2½	2½					38°	30°	25°
		45°	32°	25°	20°	3	3						37°	30°

It must be remembered that the bow or quarter table gives course alterations which will keep her *roughly on track*. She will arrive sooner or later at her next mark according to whether the current is with her (on the quarter) or against her (on the bow). Since these simple tables are for use over short distances of up to 5–8 miles between marks, when in normal conditions the marks (one or the other) will be visible for at least 4 of those miles, the actual time is less critical than staying on track. In fog the problem will have to be tackled a little more carefully, textbook fashion.

SWINGING THE COMPASS

If the owner can afford it a professional swing and compass adjustment is best on all counts; especially if he is there to watch. The prime objective is a correctly swung compass, however; interest and DIY motives come second.

Failing this the procedure isn't beyond an amateur's ability. The first priority is to position the steering compass as far away from magnetic interference as possible. One can say no more than this because a truly free position in the cockpit of a small yacht is scarcely possible. What we are after is a deviation curve of the least possible importance. The engine mass, *below* the compass, is a prime suspect and important because it can also produce heeling error, i.e. as the boat heels the mass moves out sideways and gives a lateral 'pull' that is greater than when it is directly below the compass. Look behind the bulkhead. A fire extinguisher on one side plus a cooker offers less possibility of deviation than the navigator's corner on the other side with its bulkhead-mounted echosounder, radio, hand bearing compass etc. I have heard of a transistor radio lying on a bunk ten feet away from the compass which exerted over 5° of deviation.

There is a temporary alternative if the cockpit is a regular nest of unavoidable interference and that is to mount the main compass on the main bulkhead below where it is usually well clear of trouble and have a cheap little steering compass in the cockpit. Courses and headings are checked on the safe compass and the helmsman steers to whatever heading his steering compass shows when the boat is on course.

The simplest of all swings is to take the hand bearing compass ashore and zero it (check for error anyway) by taking bearings against map or chart bearings while standing in a 'safe' area. If errors do show it will either be due to buried metal underfoot (it wasn't a 'safe' area), something about one's person (steel-rimmed spectacles?), or a mechanical fault such as pivot wear or a misaligned prism. Having absolved the HB compass from sin it can be taken aboard and used to check the yacht's steering compass. To do this it is necessary to stand exactly amidships clear of stanchions, rigging and so forth. The companionway is a good spot since the elbows can be braced while taking an exact bearing of the middle of the mast. Under low revs run the boat on a series of headings, N-S then E-W.

Using a *brass* or non-magnetic small screwdriver, adjust the appropriate magnets on the bottom of the steering compass to cancel out any anomalies. This isn't at all easy to do. Run the N-S, E-W headings again. Now run checks on NE-SW and SE-NW. If you can't get the worse deviation down to less than 5° only a professional can help you.

A swing by pelorus is the only alternative to a HB compass, and a more professional approach anyway. A pelorus (dumb compass) can be made as follows. Cut out the compass rose from an old chart and glue it on stiff card. Bend a strip of tin to form a double sight (turn both ends up at right angles) and hammer a tack through its centre, through the compass centre into a baseboard which has a fore-and-aft line on it (Fig. 58). In order to mount it high enough on the coachroof for comfortable sighting a wooden box or small stool can be lashed in place and the pelorus taped down on top with its fore-and-aft line exactly in line with the centreline of the yacht.

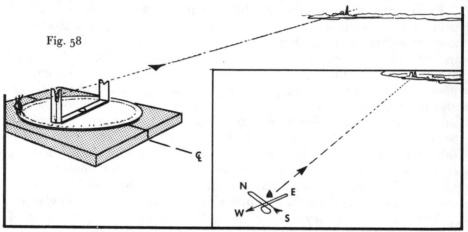

Fig. 58

Select an area which has a prominent shore object, also on the large scale chart, visible at a distance of at least 1 mile, preferably 2–3 miles. Select a permanent buoy or beacon on the chart and measure the exact magnetic bearing from it to the shore object, correcting it by updating the chart variation if necessary.

The aim now is to make the N-S and other runs as already described. For example: ship's compass heading N, pelorus card set to N on its fore-and-aft line, motor along until your buoy or nearby beacon comes into line with the distant shore mark. If the compass is accurate a sight taken by pelorus will be the same as the chart magnetic bearing. But say the chart bearing was 155° Mag. and the bearing taken by pelorus as the marks came into line showed 152°, we can note down −3° (E deviation), or if it showed 158° we'd have a +3° or W deviation.

The simplest deviation card to use is a table set out with two columns of figures.

FOR 000° STEER 003°
FOR 045° STEER 048°
FOR 090° STEER 100°   and so on.

Headings between these eight points are a matter for interpolation, or a graph can be made to give a deviation curve.

NAVIGATING BUOYED RIVERS IN FOG

		1	2	3	4	5	6	7	8	9
		SPEED IN KNOTS								
	1	6		2	1½	1¼	1	¾	¾	¾
	2	12		4	3	2½	2	1¾	1½	1¼
	3	18		6	4½	3½	3	2½	2¼	2
	4	24	12	8	6	4¾	4	3½	3	2¾
	5	30	15	10	7½	6	5	4¼	3¾	3¼
	6	36	18	12	9	7¼	6	5¼	4½	4
	7	42	21	14	10½	8½	7	6	5¼	4¾
	8	48	24	16	12	9½	8	6¾	6	5¼
	9	54	27	18	13½	10¾	9	7¾	6¾	6
	10	60	30	20	15	12	10	8½	7½	6¾

(Left axis: DISTANCE IN CABLES)

1 N.MILE = 10 CABLES

Motoring at a fixed speed, note the distance in cables from buoy to buoy. Add or subtract tidal stream (current) Rate to find Speed Over the Ground. Consult the table to find the time in minutes between buoys.

Example: Distance to next buoy is 3 cables, speed 3 knots minus 1 knot foul tide = 2 knots. Time to reach next buoy 9 minutes.

Note: Interpolate for speeds and distances involving half knots, half cables etc. For distances exceeding 1 mile multiply the 10 cable (1 n.m.) figures as necessary, e.g. 2 miles 4 cables at 4 knots = 36 minutes.

1 N. MILE = 10 CABLES.   1 CABLE = 608 FT OR 185 METRES.

LOG CALIBRATION

It is relatively simple to calibrate a log, but the actual calculations are trickier than one might expect. One might assume that it is simply a question of averaging log readings during two runs over a known distance, one upstream and one downstream to cancel out tidal effect. The snag is that if for instance a downstream run over a measured mile took 10 minutes and the upstream run took 15 minutes we'd be left with 5 minutes of tidal effect unaccounted for. The temptation is to carry out the whole operation during slack water, but this again can lead to errors since it is unlikely that there will be no stream at all.

In tidal waters, then, it is better to accept the fact that there will be current to deal with and deliberately choose a time when the current is running at a near-constant rate, half-flood or half-ebb rather than near HW or LW. In terms of our speed *through the water* tide is not a factor. The *actual* speed can be worked out from the time and distance taken over the two runs and the tidal rate at that time. By using this information and the logged distances shown for each run, the log error can be identified.

It isn't necessary to have an exact measured mile for log calibration. Any known distance (preferably using shore marks and transits) taken from the chart and of about 1 nautical mile, but certainly not less than half a mile, will do. A river is usually best since the shore is close and in the absence of good transits a course parallel to the shore is easy to follow; by sighting across the cockpit bulkhead it is simple to see when the mark is squarely on the beam.

Make two runs, one up-tide and one down-tide, noting the exact time and log reading for each. Keep to a consistent speed throughout and preferably under engine at cruising revs for this reason.

Speed, distance and tidal allowance

Divide the distance of each leg by the time taken on each occasion, add the two together and then divide by 2; this cancels out tide effect.

E.g. distance 1 nautical mile (n.m.), time 10 minutes.

Speed $= \frac{1}{10} \times 60 = 6.0$ knots DOWNSTREAM

Distance 1 n.m., Time 15 min.

Speed $= \frac{1}{15} \times 60 = 4.0$ knots UPSTREAM

Hence average speed $= \dfrac{6.0 + 4.0}{2} = 5.0$ knots

For tidal rate we simply subtract the slower of the two speeds from the faster and then divide by 2 for the average.

$$\frac{6.0 - 4.0}{2} = 1 \text{ knot tidal rate}$$

Knowing that we had a knot of tidal current, the distance that the log *should* have registered can be compared to the distance that it actually showed to find the error.

E.g.: The tidal rate is 1 knot, which means that in 10 minutes (the time of the downstream leg, remember) the tide will have run 1/6th of a nautical mile (0.17) during that time. Hence the log should read 1 n.m. minus 0.17 or 0.83 n.m. Any difference between this figure and the distance which the log actually records will be log error. For instance, if the log read 0.9 n.m. after that first leg, the error would be 0.07 n.m. (0.9 − 0.83 = 0.07 n.m.). In percentage terms this is 0.07 × 100 ÷ 0.83 = 8.4 per cent over-reading.

The same calculation carried out for the other upstream leg will confirm the error, and then an average can be taken from the two. Many modern logs can be adjusted by means of the number of turns or clicks necessary for so many per cent error, according to the maker's instructions. If you do adjust your log in this way it is wise to make further runs either at the time or on another occasion in order to check the final accuracy. In practice, any error of less than 10 per cent need not be trimmed out, provided the error is known and applied to all distances run when navigating. In the case above if we take the error to the nearest figure, e.g. 8 per cent, and apply it $\frac{100}{108}$ the correct distance run through the water will be obtained.

Another way to establish log error is to compare *actual* speed in the same way as above, with *logged* speed, i.e. the speed which was calculated from the distance which the instrument showed on the two legs and the time taken.

Using the same figures again, logged distance downstream was 0.9 n.m. and we'll assume that the distance logged upstream was 1.36 n.m. Average speed by log is then (0.9 + 1.36) ÷ (10 + 15) × 60 = 5.42 knots. Since we have already calculated the actual speed as 5 knots the error is therefore 0.42 knots or 0.42 ÷ 5 × 100 = 8.4 per cent log error, over-reading.

Using the log   Since distance recorded and speed are two quite separate functions, although both may be incorporated in the same instrument, it is important to note that both can have independent errors and so both should be checked separately. It is no bad thing either to record both speed and distance in the logbook so that in the event of an error in one the other can be used as a check.

CHAPTER IX – THE NIGHT WATCH

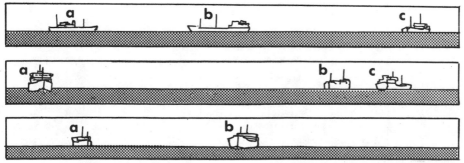

Fig. 59

EXERCISE 3

1. A and B are crossing well ahead but C is closing and converging.
2. C is receding and B should cross astern of A – which is getting dangerously close to the observer's yacht.
3. Assuming that the observer has just crossed ahead of B, vessel A, also crossing astern of B, will pose a threat to the observer's yacht.

CHAPTER X – WIND AND WAVE

BEAUFORT WIND SCALE

Deep-sea criterion. Wave forms can alter considerably in shallow waters or waters influenced by tidal currents.

Force	Knots	Description	Sea Criterion	Land Criterion	Average wave height (m)	Max. any 10 min. period
0	0–1	Calm	Mirror-like	Smoke rises vertically	—	
1	1–3	Light air	Ripples, no crests	Smoke shows direction, but not windvanes	—	
2	4–6	Light breeze	Small wavelets. Crests are glassy – not breaking.	Wind felt. Leaves rustle.	0.15	
3	7–10	Gentle breeze	Large wavelets. Crests begin to break.	Leaves and twigs in constant motion	0.5	(0.8)
4	11–16	Moderate breeze	Small waves. Fairly frequent white horses.	Dust rises, small branches move.	1.1	(1.8)
5	17–21	Fresh breeze	Moderate waves with longer form. Many white horses, some spray.	Small trees in leaf swaying.	2.0	(3.2)
6	22–27	Strong breeze	Large waves begin to form. Foam crests more extensive everywhere.	Large branches in motion. Difficulty with umbrellas.	3.1	(5.0)
7	28–33	Near gale	Sea heaps up. Foam from breaking waves blows to leeward in streaks.	Difficult to walk against. Damage to trees.	4.5	(7.2)
8	34–40	Gale	Moderately high waves of greater length. Spindrift blowing from crests. Long white streaks downwind.	Above this force there is increasing damage ashore to sheds and other buildings.	6.7	(10.7)
9	41–47	Strong gale	High waves. Crests begin to topple and roll. Spray may affect visibility.		9.3	(14.9)
10	48–55	Storm	Very high waves. Long crests overhanging. Whole surface of sea has white appearance. Tumbling of sea heavy and shock-like.		12.3	(19.7)
11	56–63	Violent storm	Exceptionally high waves. Small ships may be lost to view in troughs. Wave crests blown into froth everywhere.		15.5	(24.8)
12	64+	Hurricane	Air filled with foam and spray. Sea completely white.		?	(??)

CHAPTER XI – BIG SHIP VERSUS SMALL YACHT

EXERCISE 1

1. Stern and sidelights not seen at the same time: masthead and stern light not seen together.
2. If over 50 m length she must carry two masthead lights.
3. Two miles minimum.
4. Whether she is running, crossing your bows or reaching, her course is liable to be a collision one.
5. Two siren blasts: I am turning to PORT.
6. She is trawling as opposed to drift-netting, long-lining etc.

Appendix Two –
The 'Dry Pilot' Game

This game was devised under the cabin lamp on the long winter evenings aboard the old schooner *Hoshi* and many a time we sat around the big mahogany swinging table with the stove red-hot and the bare spars above us moaning in the bleak night wind.

'What shall we have tonight,' I would ask, opening the chart folio, 'English Channel middle sheet, Irish Sea, Southern North Sea?' The dice would roll and soon we would be absorbed in heated argument about the tidal rates off Beachy Head or whether a player could cross Chichester bar at that state of tide. For this is the beauty of the game. You use any chart and navigate by almanac and tidal stream atlas. There are endless variations that can be played, and you can formulate new rules aimed at introducing more and more realism. You get to know a chart which next year you may be using and you become slick at hunting up navigational information quickly.

Basically this is a passage race using the throw of a pair of dice to give an hourly log reading. Players hand 'Fate' cards to each other which when obeyed may either set you far off course or give you a hazardous choice to make. Alternatively, a Fate card (as in real life) can send you racing up your course line to win.

YOU WILL NEED
A pair of dice, parallel rules, dividers, an eraser and a soft pencil. A passage chart (about 7 n.m. to the inch) is ideal; an almanac and a tidal stream atlas, pilot books and some scrap paper complete the equipment.

The Cards 32 slips of stiff card about 3 × 1½ in. comprising: 1 Starting Wind card, N on one side S on the other; 18 Fate and 8 Change of Wind cards, plus 5 Wind Force cards as detailed later.

The 16 Fate cards are shuffled and divided equally between players. They include Advantage and Disadvantage cards and players may not look at them, keeping their packs face down. Players *must* get rid of all cards before reaching their destination and this is done by offering (giving him a chance pick) a card to an opponent at any time during the course of the game. Upon taking a card a player *must* comply with its instructions before counting his next throw (unless otherwise instructed).

Write on the cards as follows:

1. Look up time and height of HW at any port designated by the giver of this card. Miss one throw while doing so.

2. Fouled hull. Deduct 2 from your throw for the next three throws.

3. Log over-registers. Deduct 4 from your next throw. If less than 4 deduct balance from following throw.

4. Westerly deviation. Add your next throw and move position 10 miles to port.

5. Easterly deviation. Add your next throw and move position 10 miles to starboard.

6. Man overboard. Miss two throws.

7. Anchor at once. If depth exceeds chart soundings of 5 fathoms, heave-to for three throws, drifting to leeward and with tidal set at 2 knots. Your boat is lost if lee shore in Force 6–8.

8. Mainsail torn: Wait (miss) three throws while repairing it or sail at 2 knots with wind abaft the beam.

9. Clean hull. Add 3 to each throw for the next three throws.

10. Fair tidal eddy. Move up-tide 3 miles.

11. Ship's papers: Retain until needed. Surrendering this card (laying it aside) permits you to disregard any disadvantage card.

13. Engine card. You may use your engine for a distance of 10 consecutive miles at any time. Retain until needed, then discard.

14. Spinnaker card. Add 4 miles to each of the next three throws if the wind is abaft the beam. You may not retain this card.

15. Fog patches. The giver of this card must halve his score (or nearest figure below) for the next three throws.

16. Good RDF fix. Move 5 miles in any desired direction.

17. Attentive helmsman: Add 5 miles to your next score.

18. Bad navigation: Giver of this card must move 5 miles in any direction designated by you.

Change of Wind Cards

The North-South card used at the commencement of play according to dice (see Rules)

Eight cards: N–NE–E–SE–S–SW–W–NW

Wind Force Cards

1–2   All players count only half score (or nearest below) until the next change of wind.

3–4   All players use dice score as allowed.

5–6   All players use dice score as allowed plus 2 knots with wind abaft the beam.

6–8   All players going to windward use maximum 4 knots whatever the dice score may be.

7–9   All players heave-to and drift to leeward at 2 knots if closehauled, or run off at 6 knots bringing the wind either dead astern or 45° on either quarter.

THE RULES

Use normal chart plotting procedure and start the game by turning to the appropriate tidal information in the almanac. E.g., if at start of play it is 2 hours after HW Dover spring rates, apply tidal set and height considerations as in real life. Each round of throws equals 1 hour of tide.

1. Choose a destination port. Players start from different points on the chart of their own choosing, but at equal distances.

2. Throw one dice for starting wind (1–3 = N wind, 3–6 = S wind). Take a Force card and leave both on view. *Any player throwing a double 6 or a double 4 turns up a new Change of Wind card and a new Force card.*

3. **Offering cards**: *after complying with each card it is laid aside.*

4. Players closehauled may sail at 45° to the true wind and at a maximum of 5 knots. If they score more than this, however, they may tack and use up the balance remaining. Players with the wind abaft the beam may use a maximum of 8 knots. If they score more than this they may alter course 45° and use up the balance remaining.

5. If a player is put aground (and not wrecked) he can get off on his next throw if the tide is rising, otherwise he must wait until it has ebbed and flooded sufficiently to float his 1.5 metre draft.

6. A player may HEAVE-TO (miss a throw) whenever he pleases.

7. A player may not pass over shoal ground unless the *actual* state of tide at the time of play and the state of sea (in the opinion of the other players) allows.

8. **Winning** A player must pass the designated port entrance or agreed point. If his dice throw takes him *too far*, e.g. he cannot use up the distance thrown inside the port, he must come out again for the balance of the throw. He must then wait until he throws any double, when he is deemed to have won.

9. **Objections** One player can at any time object to the navigational decisions or seamanship of another player, who must then defend his actions satisfactorily. If no agreement can be reached the issue is decided by each throwing one dice.

OTHER VERSIONS
Any of the RORC races can be simulated by substituting different Fate cards. A Gale Warning version is also great fun. The game begins with a gale warning of Southerly Force 8 Imminent, and the Wind and Force cards are altered as follows: SE F 5–6 Vis 2 M; S F 6–7 vis ½ M; S F 7–8 vis ½ M; SW F 8–10 vis 100 metres; NW F 8–10 vis 5 M; NW F 4–5 vis unlimited.

Play starts with the wind SE F 5–6 dense drizzle, and the Wind cards are arranged in the sequence above. The Fate cards have substitutions dealing with storm conditions, rescue services etc. It is up to the players to make their own rules and cards.

STARTING TO PLAY   An example
Agree on the type of yachts and their draft, otherwise take this as being 1.5 m. Throw dice for starting wind, e.g. it might be N F 3–4. Agree on destination port and declare your starting points as in Rule 1. *Note*: it adds a bit of a gamble if the wind is decided *after* players have proclaimed their starting points. Check tidal state in almanac.

The game may then proceed something like this. Player 1 throws 4–2 but being closehauled can only use 5 unless he tacks to use up the balance.

Player B throws double 6. He takes a Change of Wind card and a Force card, SW F 1–2. His opponent also asks him to take a Fate card: Clean hull adds 3. He now has the wind free and a total of 15 to be used, but he can only use 8 miles of this in a straight line. Being in the mouth of a river he cannot alter course 45° to use the balance but the tidal atlas tells him that he has a 4 knot tide under him. He can therefore step off 8 + 4 = 12 along his course line.

Player A is now hard on the wind. He throws 10 but can only use 5 unless he tacks. He tacks up-tide thus lee-bowing it for the balance count of 5. (And so forth.)